TALES FROM TANZANIA

A mostly true story

By

Scott Balows

This book is a work of non-fiction. Names and places have been changed to protect the privacy of all individuals. The events and situations are true.

ISBN: 1-4140-0396-X (e-book)
ISBN: 1-4140-0395-1 (Paperback)

This book is printed on acid-free paper.

1stBooks – rev. 01/16/04

To my parents, for giving me a love of travel—and a few other things.

Thanks to April Speed for designing the cover,
and to Michael Zitt for his help.

Here it is, friends: the highlights of my African journal. A collection of moments, observations and images that stood out. Mostly amusing. Occasionally educational. Rarely boring or sentimental. And like a Tanzanian winter, long and dry. Enjoy.

DAY 1

Victoria Falls, Zimbabwe to Nairobi, Kenya

There is a monkey at the next table. He just hopped up there; now he sits a few feet away from me and reaches for a plate of leftover fruit. This is one particular monkey: He evaluates the free slice of melon with the keen eye of a produce inspector before popping it into his mouth. He likes it.

In the background, the low rumble of Victoria Falls thunders as it plunges 300 feet into a nearby gorge, sending streams of mist above the tallest trees. This is my last day here, and I am about to leave for the airport and start a Tanzanian safari. I have been traveling around Zimbabwe and Botswana with some friends from Chicago for the past two weeks, but now I'm dining alone on the grassy terrace of the Ilala Lodge.

I point out the freeloading monkey to the nearest waiter, but he only nods and smiles as if to say, "Yes. You have correctly identified a monkey." According to the guidebook, the agile simian with the grayish-green body and the long tail is a vervet, which often grows fearless around hotels and campgrounds and can become a nuisance if allowed to forage tableside. As part of his complete breakfast, the monkey picks at a half-eaten muffin and slurps milk from a bowl of cereal. Finished with his table, he stands on his haunches to get a better look at what I'm having and appraises my

1

buffet selection. He appears to weigh the implications of hopping over here now that he's cleaned his plate, and our eyes lock as I take a slow-motion bite of fresh fruit.

This is when it hits me that I am no longer on a well-supervised Zambezi River trip with my buddies from Chicago. I am traveling through The Dark Continent, alone. The butterflies in my stomach are almost the size of kori bustards, Africa's heaviest flying birds, which tip the scales at a whopping 42 pounds. According to the guidebook, the kori bustard prefers open country and strides across the savanna searching for lizards, insects and seeds. His call is a resonant, ominous "oooom." A voice inside my head makes this sound just as the vervet makes a false charge for my mango.

My adventure begins two weeks earlier with a river safari above Victoria Falls, and for three days, I paddle an inflatable kayak around pods of hippos through crocodile-infested waters. Our armed guide, Peter—a pale, redheaded cross between John Wayne and John Cleese—keeps the group in a state of bemused panic with cautionary tales of belligerent hippos tipping canoes and a crocodile that once leaped into a passenger's lap. That encounter happened just a few weeks before my arrival, on this same stretch of river, when a croc launched out of the water and bit down on a startled tourist's kayak. He chomped into the bow with a toothy grin—narrowly missing the front paddler's toes—and several dozen puncture wounds ruptured at once. The kayak seeped air like spewing blood and deflated into a crumpled, yellow nub. Pieces of shredded rubber were tangled in the croc's mouth as he thrashed around to free himself, and the brief distraction gave the passengers just enough time to flee the sinking raft and swim to the nearest shore.

"To a croc, your craft looks just like a dead, floating hippo," Peter says. "He thought he might have an easy meal."

"Great. We look like crocodile food," I say to Mitch, my paddling partner.

"You'll know the craft," Peter says. "It's the one with all the patches on the bow."

Mitch inspects our two-man kayak and is no longer excited about sitting in front.

"Yep. It's covered in patches," he says.

"Well, if a croc bites into this kayak, I will crap my pants with such force, it will repel it," I assure Mitch, who thinks that will be an effective deterrent.

We don't believe crocodiles have elephant memories but plan on staying close to the guide, since he has the gun. Before paddling down the river on the first day, Peter quiets our group and delivers The Hippo Safety Orientation. He explains that the Zambezi is home to many pods of the territorial herbivores, and they will not hesitate to attack a kayak.

"Should your craft suddenly erupt three meters out of the water, you are not capsizing," Peter says in a clipped British accent. "You have encountered an angry hippo."

Peter delivers his speech in deliberate bursts of emphasis, but his animated voice defangs the gravity of his serious words.

"Do not attempt to save your loved ones. Do not retrieve your sentimental college cap."

In his matching forest-green ranger shirt and thigh-high shorts, Peter resembles a character from a Monty Python sketch. Almost anything said in a British accent sounds funny to me, and I cannot help but snicker at inappropriate moments during the potentially lifesaving speech.

"Swim away from your craft as quickly as you can toward the shore or the other kayaks that are swiftly vacating the area," Peter says. "Do not take this personally. The hippo is not angry at you. He is angry at your craft."

The folly of paddling what is essentially a sturdy pool toy down a river filled with large animals who either a) don't like us or b) think we're food is casually dismissed, and we launch our inflatable kayaks onto the upper Zambezi. A sandy hump of tree-covered island splits the river in two, and Peter leads us down a narrow channel. We are on the river only a short time before we encounter our first pod.

"Yesterday, a pod of hippos was up ahead," he says. "If they are still here, stay in single file. Do not stop. Stay close to the shoreline. And whatever you do, keep moving."

There they are, just as he said: More than half a dozen hippos are sunning themselves on a nearby beach. In spite of their awkward shape and stumpy legs, hippos can actually spring to their feet quite nimbly. They hop right up, snorting-mad and tossing their heads about. They would appear to be angry at our crafts.

"Single file, please," Peter says. "Stay close to the shoreline."

The group clusters along the shore—the same shore as the hippos—and paddles quickly to form a single chain of pointed rafts.

"Keep moving," Peter continues. "Do not stop. The hippos will enter the water."

He is right again. One by one, the hippos begrudgingly head to the river's edge and splash into the water like pinkish-brown submarines. Some of the angry hippos are now in the water with us, and one cannot help but notice that *some angry hippos are now in the water with us.*

"Hey, Mitch, why is this so much better than having them on the shore?" I ask. "Didn't that seem a lot better?"

"Keep moving please. Keep moving," Peter yells, the strain and urgency of his voice increasing.

The group paddles steadily, hugging the shoreline and banging our kayaks with our paddles to drive the remaining hippos into the water. Several hippos have yet to enter as the lead kayak nears the annoyed pod. The passengers choose this inopportune moment to stop paddling and retrieve their cameras for a few Kodak moments.

"Keep moving," yells Peter. "Don't stop."

While they fumble with their Nikons, their kayak meanders toward shore and is soon perpendicular to the beach. They stop.

"This is not a good time to fuck up," says Peter.

But it is too late. The kayak behind them is unable to stop in time and broadsides their craft. Mitch and I cannot paddle backward fast enough so we rear-end the second raft, and soon a pileup of inflatable kayaks forms a traffic jam along the shores of the Zambezi River.

Peter shouts instructions. Surly hippos splash into the river. Mini oil wells gush from the surface as the hippos exhale, and we wait for someone's kayak to shoot three meters out of the water. If a hippo gets angry at our craft, I know I will be the guy who tries to retrieve his sentimental college cap.

"He tried to retrieve his college cap," my friend T.S. will have to inform my parents. "That's when the hippo got him."

"He said he was going to crap his pants," Mitch will add, regrettably.

There is a delicious irony in being eaten by a vegetarian, but the hippos let us pass without capsizing anyone, and my favorite hat and I continue downstream. A worn-out Peter herds us through the narrow channel and into the main flow where the river widens.

"There are hippos to the left of us," he says, "and crocodiles to the right."

In spite of being this low on the food chain, and having large predators on either side of us, as well as questionable paddling skills, the group breaks the tension with a snippet of improvised song.

"Hippos to the left of me, crocodiles to the right, here I am, stuck in the middle with you," we sing. "Stuck in the middle with you."

A week of whitewater rafting beneath Victoria Falls follows, and on this leg we paddle 16-foot rafts over house-size waves with considerable enthusiasm and occasional finesse. Crocodiles and hippos live here too, so the guides encourage us to remain inside the rafts at all times. Their sensible instructions go unheeded one evening about halfway through the trip.

The Chicago Gang is paddling with a sturdy American guide, also named Peter. Our day begins with a long portage: Half a dozen rafts are hauled across a slick, rocky shoreline and hooked up to a makeshift pulley system of ropes and sunburned shoulders. Perched on the slippery edge of a watery death, we lower each raft down the jagged edge of a rushing waterfall. The rafts are unwieldy, and we have to balance on wet rocks above a three-story drop to ease them into the river. The task's completion is marked by a helmet-rattling, 30-foot cliff jump into an assuredly predator-free section of the river, followed by a brisk swim to the nearby rafts. The portage takes so long, though, that the sun has set by the time the group floats to our next campsite, and we paddle blindly through a dark canyon.

The roar of upcoming rapids signals another Class V section of the river, and we brace ourselves for an unseen impact. Wet thunder rumbles between the narrow walls, and the volume indicates something nasty and drenching. The rumble grows louder and the raft pitches upward. A wall of water crashes into our faces, and a staircase of rollicking wave trains bounces us down the river. We navigate the watery peaks by the moon's shifting glow and are spat out upright into a calm stretch of water. The river makes a hard turn, and an outcrop forms a massive eddy that causes the current to go in the opposite direction of the main flow. The circulating water creates a boiling whirlpool, and our raft is sucked into its thick-fingered grasp.

"Paddle hard! Paddle hard! Dig! Dig! Dig!" yells Peter.

The group paddles hard to dig through the eddy line and enter the main flow, but the current overpowers us and drags the raft toward shore. Drained after our failed burst of energy and humbled by the awesome power of the river, we catch our breath for a moment and regroup with a few words of encouragement from Peter. On the second attempt, our oars slice into the water and propel the raft against the flow. I am paddling in front, on the right side of the raft, where it first encounters the eddy line. The opposing currents meet here in a swirling vortex, and the suction drags my corner of the raft beneath the surface. The front compartment floods with churning water, and the whirlpool sucks on my paddle, yanking me into the froth like a giant invisible hand.

This is unfortunate: I am no longer inside the raft but in Africa, in a crocodile-infested river, at night. Sputtering, my head breaks the surface and I gulp for air. The raft is gone, and I wait for the "not responsible for death or dismemberment" clause in the trip waiver to take effect. I consider unleashing my Crapping Defense Tactics against any crocodiles, but my weaponry has been rendered inoperative: I am scared shitless.

Spinning around, I see the raft. It has been pulled back into the eddy, about 15 feet in front of me. The yellow inflatable tubes seem very distant, and I kick for the life preserver that is Peter's outstretched hand, certain that dozens of crocs are on their way to investigate the disturbance. Suddenly, I am yanked toward the raft as Peter grabs my hand and Mitch pulls me toward the bow. I launch myself inside with minimal encouragement and dive headfirst onto the floor, inches ahead of a hungry croc that snaps down on my ankles and catches a mouthful of bubbles, I'm almost positive. Exhausted and shaky after the seven-second ordeal, I regain a seat and gape at my friends in disbelief.

"Are you OK?" asks Penn.

"Don't ever do that again," says Mitch, but I can only nod and pant heavily.

We muscle our way out of the eddy on the third attempt and paddle toward a dark camp. After heart-stopping rides like that, our final few days in Botswana's Chobe National Park at an open-air lodge are a well-deserved respite. Our thatched-roof chalets are perched on a thickly wooded slope overlooking a watering hole and an epic plain, and the guides chauffeur us around in oversize jeeps with bleacher seating. We photograph lion prides and drink gin and tonics at sunset while bobbing brown periscopes reveal families of elephants swimming across the Chobe River.

The Chicago Gang splits up here: Penn and T.S. stay an extra day in the park, and their Land Rover disappears down a road in a cloud of dust. Mitch and I return to Victoria Falls, where he begins his long journey back to the States.

This leaves me eating breakfast alone at the Ilala Lodge, except for the monkey, who appears moments away from joining me.

I ease my chair back from the table so as not to startle him and begin Part II of my African vacation: a Tanzanian safari with visits to the Serengeti plains, Ngorongoro Crater and the foothills of Mt. Kilimanjaro. These places even sound as though someone will be eaten by a croc or attacked by a monkey during breakfast. Gore 'n' gore. Kill-a-man. The names conjure primal, violent settings and outcomes that are bloodied and uncertain. All I know for sure is that for the next two weeks, I will be driving across Tanzania in a big truck with a bunch of strangers. Let's hope nobody gets hurt.

     After checking out of the hotel, I exit the lobby and walk toward the airport shuttle. The smiling, gap-toothed porter hefts my duffel bag and stores it inside the van. I've stayed here four times in the past two weeks, so he knows me by name, and we see each other off like old friends. Without warning, a stealthy gust of wind bursts into the hotel's courtyard and roars across the parking lot, shaking the trees and rattling the branches. As I'm about to place a foot inside the van, a cloudburst of small dry petals rains down from the tree overhead and drenches me in a confetti downpour. The leaves collect in my hat and the folds of a safari shirt, leaving a golden puddle around my feet. The astonished expression on the porter's face leaves no doubt that he thinks I am some sort of deity and that my tip will be a big one.

     The shuttle drops me off at the airport, and my first flight taxis down the runway. From the air, the mist created by Victoria Falls resembles a small village in winter, with smoky ribbons curling into the sky like dozens of chimney fires. Briton David Livingston made the falls famous when he stumbled upon them in 1855, and he named them after his favorite queen. The locals already had a name for them: *Mosai-oa-Tunya,* which means "the smoke that thunders."

The thundering smoke disappears behind the plane's left wing and we angle toward Harare, the capital of Zimbabwe. Angry locals have been slaughtering white farmers nearby, so I will not be tilling the soil during my layover; I don't have a farm in Africa. I stay inside the terminal instead and pick yellow leaves out of my shirt while studying a Swahili/English dictionary.

This is my first delusion of the trip: that I will master another language during the connecting flight.

Deep into Lesson 2—where it's learned that *jambo* means "Hello, now please speak to me in English," and a *choo* is a toilet—the plane departs for Nairobi, Kenya, and arrives at the Jomo Kenyatta International Airport without incident. The incident occurs shortly thereafter. I grab my luggage, proceed through customs and hail a cab into the city. But when I tell the cabbie my destination, he shakes his head and moans. My hotel selection causes him great sadness, and he does not wish to take me there.

"Oh no. The Hotel Boulevard is very bad," the driver assures me, "very, very bad."

He feels strongly that a different hotel would be more to my liking and he will take me there instead, now. When I insist upon staying at the prearranged, prepaid destination, he is not happy. The cabbie is missing out on a hefty commission of some sort, so midway through the trip to my hotel he raises the already agreed-upon fare. We argue.

"You can't change the fare," I say.

"You pay twelve hundred shillings," he says, flashing a chipped tooth in a crooked smile.

"You said a thousand."

"It is twelve hundred now."

"You can't do that."

"You pay twelve hundred."

"*Mwizi!*" I say, that being one of the few words retained from my brief Swahili tutorial. "*Mwizi! Mwizi!*" I continue, wagging an index finger with presidential fervor.

In this context, "*Mwizi! Mwizi!*" means "You can't change the already agreed-upon fare midway through the trip to the hotel." Technically, it means "Thief! Thief!" The cabbie is mildly amused by my worldly command of his native tongue, perhaps because my delivery sounds suspiciously like Sherman Hemsley yelling at his wife in *The Jeffersons*.

"*Mwizi! Mwizi!*"

He does not feel threatened. We split the difference.

At the Hotel Boulevard, there are warnings not to leave the hotel. Not to let a camera dangle loosely. Not to resemble a tourist walking around alone at night. Even some of the locals mock Nairobi as "Nairobbery" for the fearless street crime. Only a few years ago, Osama bin Laden bombed the American embassy here. On CNN

International, the anchor reports of a nearby marketplace going up in flames and riot police firing tear gas to disperse an unruly mob.

I felt safer on the Zambezi River, when my biggest concern was being pinned underwater against a rock by a Class V rapid. Or falling out of the raft and being eaten by a hungry crocodile. Or being smacked in the face with a big paddle. This city is dangerous. Remaining on the hotel grounds until the shuttle bus leaves for Tanzania tomorrow is starting to sound like a good idea. This part of the trip has always been intended as an intermission, and after two weeks camping on the Zambezi, a few extra hours in a real bed will not be turned down.

The hotel has other diversions, including a popular pool, swift Internet access and a sunny outdoor bar shaded by a thatched roof. Within minutes, my beer allegiance shifts from Zambezi Lager to Tusker Beer, Kenya's heritage since 1922. Or maybe 1923. No one seems quite certain, and the date varies on every label I inspect. Tusker Beer was named, surprisingly, in honor of an elephant that went on a rampage and fatally wounded one of the brewery's founders. An unusual way to commemorate a killer pachyderm, but a refreshing lager nonetheless.

I spend the afternoon doing laundry in the bathroom sink and hanging damp clothes on the hotel balcony. In the computer room adjacent to the pool, the first trip dispatches are e-mailed home and parents and friends are notified of the Chicago Gang's relatively safe passage down the Zambezi River. I claim a lounge chair next to the empty pool and recline in the equatorial sun with my book for the trip: *Hannibal*, Thomas Harris's sequel to *The Silence of the Lambs*.

I can hardly believe that I'm at the Hotel Boulevard in downtown Nairobi, in a chair by the pool, while my laundry dries and the traffic whizzes by, reading *Hannibal*. Serious acclimation is required, mostly in the form of another Tusker. A few lagers later, the chairs are full and the pool area could be mistaken for the United Nations Country Club at happy hour. French, German, Japanese, Indian, Swahili, Spanish, English and Australian accents intermingle into one indecipherable tongue. The busy waiter tells me that these folks are mostly ex-pats, and this pool is their oasis in the bustling city.

Occasionally, while reading *Hannibal*, I have to stop and remind myself that I've just paddled down the Zambezi and now I'm in downtown Nairobi relaxing in a chair by the pool, surrounded by international Tusker drinkers. My natural response is to shake my head and laugh aloud. The neighboring sunbather who recognizes my choice of reading material—and is certain I find cannibalistic doctors amusing—scowls at me.

Thoroughly baked, I return to the hotel room to repack my luggage for the second leg of the trip. This would be tough sober; slightly Tuskered, I can not determine which T-shirt goes best with khaki, and thinning the herd of excess gear takes longer than it should. This is when I discover that my new Leatherman—the unrivaled pair of industrial-strength pliers—is missing. It's gone. The handy tool was hardly even used. The contents of my duffel are dumped onto the bed and hand-searched, but it is nowhere to be found.

The Leatherman was last seen at the Ilala Lodge, where it probably disappeared under the bed or in the folds of a sheet. With a variety of useful implements, including a knife, a couple of screwdrivers, a fish scaler and tweezers—for removing stubborn lion incisors—the Leatherman was the final element in the packing puzzle. I was depending on them. The plan was to sleep inside the tent with the pliers close to my sleeping bag and use them in case of nocturnal animal attacks. In fact, several minutes were spent reading the instructions and determining which tools would be the most lethal. I even practiced finding the Leatherman in the dark. But somehow, the versatile camping accessory has escaped, proving just how resourceful and clever it truly is.

This is the second delusion of the trip: that I will fend off Africa's largest predators with my Leatherman. Perhaps I will pluck them to death.

DAY 2

Nairobi, Kenya to Arusha, Tanzania

A resonant and violent splashing echoes down the narrow, tiled hallway that leads to the hotel lobby. It sounds like reverse gargling, followed by sludge pouring into a bucket of water. A woman is in her bathroom, clinging to the toilet, nauseous. Hers is a prolonged, pained ejection, and my stomach twists in phantom sympathy. Ugh. I cringe and walk faster to put some distance between her door and me, thinking the sound alone might be contagious.

Nairobi isn't in the best of health either. Our outfitter's bus arrives in the hotel's driveway and takes two dozen passengers through the city in the morning rush hour, past aged high-rises and shafts of dirty sunlight. The downtown area is a metropolitan contradiction, with uninspired buildings and landscaped parks. Litter clings to the gutters, and the streets are lined with gated, padlocked storefronts.

To compensate for the drab views, the locals on their way to work are dressed as if on the way to job interviews. Everyone looks sharp. The women are particularly stunning, all knotted scarves and defiance, and navigate the city with supermodel authority. Nairobi's crowded sidewalks are mirrored by the busy streets, which are flooded with tourists. Large herds of outfitters escape the city at once, and dozens of vans, minivans, camper vans, buses and Land Rovers

17

surround our large bus. The shuttle migration continues south, and the traffic slows to a crawl.

In the lane next to ours, a man pulls alongside with an elaborate, erector-set ricksha of metal tubes hauling onions and potatoes. He burrows in with the intensity of an ox and launches from a crouching position. As the cart rolls along, the weight of the vegetables lifts the man off the road, and he air-pedals as furiously as a cartoon character who has just run off a cliff. The man soars repeatedly as the traffic shuffles along, working the handles with a gymnast's flair and always landing within inches of crashing into the van in front of him. The writing on the ricksha's side aptly names him. He is Sky Guy #18.

To drive the six hours from Nairobi to Arusha, Tanzania, is to travel backward through time, then forward again, but not all the way to the present. Nairobi thins out, and the crumbling foundations of cement-block suburbia are left behind. Tin-roof towns plastered in ads for Tusker Beer give way to thatched-hut villages with mud-walled homes stitched together by tree parts and cow dung. In one town, half a dozen ostriches forage through a trash heap. In a village, alongside a river, a patchwork quilt of wet clothes dries atop sun-warmed rocks.

The shuttle bus follows a paved two-lane highway across the Athi River and enters a landscape of thirsty sagebrush and lonesome trees. Dozens of Maasai women and young children tend herds of goats and cows along the roadside. Their shorn heads and graceful necks rise above blood-red shoulder cloaks, called *shulas,* and long legs emerge from beneath the rippling blankets. The Maasai carry themselves like royalty, with a muscled elegance and an unflinching dignity, a tribute to their proud reputations. The women do most of the work here: They look after the kids, milk the cows, repair the huts, prepare the food, travel many miles to fetch water and walk doubled over from the burden of great bundles of firewood. Even hunched over, with sticks on their backs, the women look regal.

In between the small towns and smaller villages where the Maasai graze their herds are long stretches of a parched, desolate country. The Athi Plains are passed on the right side of the map, and the Kaputei Plains on the left. We drive over the Maparasha Hills and through the Amboselli Game Reserve without seeing any game. Occasionally, we pass a tree.

In the distance, enormous wind spouts spin drunken paths along either side of the highway, bounding across the horizon's edge like dancing silos. One comes to life near the bus: It is a charmed cobra of wind and brown earth that rises from the ground, spirals into a giant column and punctures the sky. The twister cuts a swath wider than a herd of stampeding elephants and parallels the shuttle. It stirs up clouds of dust and rattles the solitary trees, stripping off leaves and snapping branches. Resembling a chase scene from a killer-wind-spout movie, the twister stalks the bus down the highway. It bears down on us, obscuring the back window and clipping our fender. The tourists look on anxiously as the spout pursues us in a mad dash across Kenya, wondering if we're in any danger of being whisked off to The Emerald City. The driver speeds up just to be safe.

   A clipboard is passed around for the passengers to write down their names, passport numbers, birthdays, specific safaris and countries of origin. The answers reveal that most everyone is from the U.K. Our outfitter is a British company, and it seems the only American who has ever heard of them is me. While I'm jotting down my yellow fever vaccination certification number, a van pulls alongside the bus in the next lane. A man and a woman sit in the back and relax in plush chairs with enough legroom for spacious game reserves. Snug, multicolored shorts highlight ample waists and suggest they might be countrymen. A logo on the van's door identifies their outfitter as the legendary Abercrombie & Kent, and our shuttle's elevated seating allows me a brief glimpse inside their privileged world.

   Abercrombie & Kent is safari travel at its most luxurious. Their camping excursions are shamelessly decadent, ridiculously elegant affairs. When the guests aren't staying in the priciest lodges, they sleep inside sultan-worthy tents on ostrich down—filled mattresses with 500-count linens. Their tents have private washrooms with perfumed soaps and foyers with Persian throw rugs. Porters fill basins of hot water every morning for washing, and the guides don official vests with tastefully designed nametags. In the afternoons, they snack on tea and crumpets. Before game viewing, their animals are groomed: The lion manes are highlighted; the zebra tails are shampooed and blow-dried.

I am not traveling with A&K. My outfitter's more reasonable prices help explain the cramped conditions on this bus. Having a window seat is a bonus, but that provides only the illusion of room. Limited legroom was available when the group boarded—but in the aisle. Additional passengers arrived later, extra seats folded out and our aisle disappeared. Now we sit four abreast, our knees as cramped as a pod of hippos sharing a sleeping bag.

Meanwhile, on the A&K van, they're enjoying cheese and grapes from a silver tray.

The bus stops at a gas station near the Kenyan border. An ancient Maasai woman stands nearby, draped in colorful necklaces and a bright *shula*. Her face is a topographical map of narrow, weathered lines, and her hair is pulled back in a wiry gray bun. Leathery hands clutch a wooden tray filled with bracelets, rings and other jewelry, and she shuffles alongside the bus offering up the beaded souvenirs. This is my first close-up of a Maasai woman, and as my gaze reaches her ears, I am riveted. The Maasai take enormous pride in stretching giant holes in their ears, and this woman must be greatly admired. Her ears are masterpieces of lobe augmentation and resemble thick, misshapen slices of Swiss cheese. They have a variety of holes that a quartet of brides could use to size engagement rings and earrings that resemble inverted wedding cakes. The weight of the

21

multitiered jewelry causes the tops of her ears to droop away from her head, halfway to a shoulder. With a strong updraft, she could be The Flying Maasai. By the time she reaches my window and offers up her tray, my mouth hangs open. I grab for an ear—my own. Instantaneous Phantom Ear Pain strikes without warning.

The shuttle crosses the border into Tanzania, East Africa's largest country (about twice the size of California), and drives south toward Arusha. This part of the country appears to be the victim of a 100-year drought but miraculously segues into a veritable Eden: the lush, green foothills that flank Mt. Meru, the country's second-highest peak.

Arusha is the safari capital of Tanzania, and our shuttle arrives at a hotel crowded with buses and vans. Centered inside the parking lot is an area cordoned off by a chain-link fence topped with barbed wire; wrought iron gates manned by armed, uniformed guards mark the entrance. Just as we're wondering what this is for, the gates open and the guards usher us inside with a nod of their automatic weapons. This cage is ours.

The shuttle drives inside the enclosure and the gates are locked behind us. On first glance, it appears that we have driven into a riot: Hundreds of local men circle the perimeter yelling and gesturing at us. Two dozen tourists disembark, while the men behind the fence wave snacks, souvenirs, newspapers and safari signs. Two men scale the roof of our shuttle, untie a large canvas tarp and begin tossing our luggage to the ground. The tourists make mad dashes to catch their bags before they hit the pavement, as though they packed fine china and not just khaki.

"Tanzanian Explorer," I say to an official-looking man with a clipboard.

He is matching guests with guides and signals to mine. A man approaches and flashes me with a wide, blinding smile. He resembles a young Robert Guillaume, from *Benson*, but in an extra-large baseball cap. His wiry frame carries a uniform of a weathered T-shirt and faded blue jeans. He is nametag-free.

"Jambo," I say.

"Jambo," says Kinyua.

"I'm Scott from Chicago."

"Hello. I'm Kinyua," he says. "Welcome to Tanzania. This way to the truck. OK? All right."

Clutching my luggage, I follow Kinyua out of the fenced-in enclosure, past the spirited sales pitches of several dozen men and toward a large truck. A small flight of stairs leads me to the back of an enormous vehicle, the All-Wheel-Drive Bedford. I am introduced to Thomas, our amiable driver, who is a tall, athletic guy with taut forearms highlighting defined veins. He has a closely shaved head and a grin that looks as though he just heard a good joke.

Juma is our cook for the trip and Thomas's mirror opposite. He is short and solid, and barely mouths hello. He appears serious and businesslike; having to cook three meals a day for a dozen people probably has that effect. Even their clothes take opposite directions:

Scott Balows

Thomas is safari casual in sneakers, blue jeans and a green T-shirt. Juma is dressed for Sunday school, with black pants, dress shoes and a short-sleeved, V-neck shirt.

Kinyua relaxes into the cushioned seat and gives an overview of the surrounding area. This part of the city is distinguished by a large number of furniture stores, lumberyards and bars. Last decade's La-Z-Boys sit in clusters along the roadside, adjacent to hefty stacks of two-by-fours and men tipping bottles of beer.

"We'll meet the rest of the group in the hotel lobby at seven o'clock," Kinyua says. "OK? All right."

The truck turns onto a wide, paved boulevard that leads to the hotel, a 12-story cement obelisk down the street from the bars. I ask Kinyua if it's OK to walk into town and patronize one of the outdoor drinking establishments, but he encourages me not to leave the hotel. Not to let a camera dangle loosely. Not to resemble a tourist walking around alone at night.

In the restaurant at the hotel in Arusha, honeymooners from Chicago sit at the next table, and we discover one degree of separation: a guy I used to work with. Lunch is ordered, and my beer allegiance shifts from Tusker Beer to Castle Lager without fanfare. While the hotel staff tidies the restaurant for that evening's dinner, I move to the adjacent bar and finish another chapter of *Hannibal*. One of the book's creepiest parts involves a plot to create genetically altered pigs. A strange, vengeful man is crossbreeding a variety of ferocious hogs to produce a super pig with an appetite for human flesh. Coming face-to-face with man-eating boars out here would be ill-timed, particularly without my trusty Leatherman. After reading another chapter, I meet Kinyua in the hotel lobby to wait for the group. This is the most anxious part of any trip: when I discover whom chance and fate have thrown me together with for the next two weeks. I hope they're nice.

A bus pulls in front of the hotel, and more than a dozen weary strangers trudge down the stairs, through the revolving door and into the high-ceilinged reception area. A mountain of duffels and sleeping bags forms inside the lobby, and the desk clerks spring into action. I watch the group enter, sizing them up, making instant decisions as to whether or not I like them. Appears to be a decent bunch: several obvious couples, a handful of unaccompanied women, a few guys.

Then a handsome and sprightly older woman with a bonnet of graying hair spins out of the revolving door. She looks exactly like the Queen of England, only smiling. It is her, or her twin. Mentally, I place extravagant headwear atop her and am convinced: Queen Elizabeth II is on my safari. I would have pegged the scion of the Windsor line as more of an Abercrombie & Kent guest myself, but here she is, traveling incognito and mingling with the common folk. To assist in her cover, QE2 wishes to be addressed as "Evelyn" and is accompanied by her "son" Roy, probably a royal butler or something.

The rest of the group spans the globe. The guests are from Canada, Switzerland, Australia and the Netherlands, but most hail from Great Britain, 9 of the 16 guests. I have trained decades for this encounter. My sense of humor was culled from watching *Monty Python's Flying Circus* every Wednesday night, beginning in junior high; *The Holy Grail* was a frequent stop on the midnight movie circuit. This conditioned me from an early age to believe that saying something in a British accent makes it funnier. This trip will be a two-week live sketch.

"You find the bar yet?" asks Brian after we are introduced.

"Up the stairs and to the right," I say, laughing already.

Brian and Trevor are two blokes from southern England. Strap an AK-47 over Brian's shoulder and he could inquire at central casting regarding any future mercenary auditions. He has grizzled features accented by a long bandanna and a safari vest, and is probably on Her Majesty's Secret Service. He looks to be in his 50s, with a buzzed head and crinkly eyes glinting from a well-traveled face. His mate Trevor looks as though he's been in a fight. He has a black hole where a front tooth should be and a giant, wartlike knot that erupts from beneath one eyebrow. He is over six feet tall, and his spiky, unkempt hair makes him appear even taller. These two look like scrappy, self-sufficient guys and are from Cornwall, which to the urban Brits is a U.K. version of West Virginia; they make occasional inbreeding jokes about them, that sort of thing.

Tony and Selena, a married couple in their late 20s, live outside London and sit next to me at the welcome dinner. Selena is a striking woman with well-toned arms and wispy blonde hair that hangs past her shoulders. Her husband resembles a young Steve

McQueen, with a blunt, scalp-hugging haircut. He has a serious demeanor but counters it with a sarcastic wit.

"The older woman," I say, nodding my head toward one end of the table, "that's Queen Elizabeth, right?"

Tony and Selena assure me that Evelyn is not the Queen of England, which leads me to believe that they are part of her entourage.

"No, she'd be wearing the khaki tiara," says Tony. "The one with the mosquito netting."

Within a few minutes of meeting me, Tony and Selena are already commenting on how smart I am. Everything I do is brilliant. The simplest tasks are successfully completed and they act as though I've just created cold fusion in my Castle Lager. Then they want to drink. I like them immediately.

"Brilliant," says Selena as I pass the butter without knocking any glasses over. "Cheers."

Janet and Tim are another well-traveled, quick-witted couple, but they're from Leeds. Janet is a rosy-cheeked redhead who looks more Irish than British. She's brash and outgoing and reminds me of Tracy Ullman.

"We have a Yank on the trip?" asks Janet, who is quick to place my flat, nasal accent. "That's lovely. Tim, Scott's from the States. What do you do there?"

"I make up ads."

"Oh, do you write the little captions?"

"Yes."

Janet thinks that is lovely, too. Her husband is a lanky, athletic fellow with dark hair and a preppy cut. He seems to be a decent guy and is assuredly slim and tall. Tim has a distinguished face, anchored by a prominent nose and a sharp jaw, and could find casting work as a young prep-school headmaster.

Roy, the royal butler, has a hairline that starts even further back than mine does, but he balances out his bare dome with a full beard that lends him a wise and hallowed demeanor. Put a brown full-length frock on him and he could pass for a friendly monk. He is practically jovial as he follows his "mum" around and tends to her needs.

Sarah and Susan are introduced to me at the same time. They are both tall—taller than I am—and about the same age, mid 20s. Sarah is a chunky blonde with a disobedient bob of blonde hair and a London tan. She reminds me of a British Drew Barrymore, with a lopsided, sleepy smile and a giggle that is a frequent part of her vocabulary.

Susan is nervous and pretty, with a boyish brown haircut and glasses that make her appear studious and thoughtful. She is from Switzerland.

"So where in Switzerland do you live?" I ask Susan.

"Outside Geneva," she says.

"It's very pretty there. I went with my parents when I was a kid. They have a big lake, right?" I say.

"Yes."

"Is this your first time to Africa?"

"Yes."

English is her second language, so she appears a little reserved around the thickly accented Brits and the rambling American. I have trouble understanding her at dinner, and we have several confused conversations that end in awkward nodding.

"Der in tu tates are you frond?" she asks me, I think.

"Yes."

Judith is not from London but sounds British to me.

"I'm from Australia," she says. "Sydney. Can you not tell the difference between an Australian accent and a British one?"

"I guess not," I say, but I'm willing to learn.

Judith seems like a cool girl. She's laid-back and funky, with shoulder-length reddish-brown hair and a slender figure. She sports the trip's first fashion statement: a small Maasai blanket as a head wrap worn beneath a floppy floral hat.

Minouk is another adventurous woman traveling solo. She has a rounded face with cherubic features, and a black ponytail as thick as a zebra's that hangs almost to her waist. She is petite; her duffel bag is almost bigger than she is.

Marc and Valerie are two French-Canadians from Quebec. Marc has a shaved head that tapers to a sharp chin and deep-set eyes beneath thick, animated brows. Valerie, in a pith helmet and wire-rimmed glasses, looks as though she just walked off the set of *Little House on the Savanna*. Midway through our first conversation, they begin speaking to each other in French.

There is another man traveling alone: Steve, an older bloke. Jowly, late 50s. We are introduced, and I catch every fourth or fifth word. He articulates with the clarity of Keith Richards on a bender and resembles a disheveled Michael Caine—if you inflated him and let the air out but had the same amount of skin left. Clone the guy and you can almost muster a full set of teeth. At the welcome dinner, he does not join the group but opts for a small table by himself. To use a British expression, the guy seems daft. Out of it. Spacey. He will be known as "The Daft One." Around dessert, he lurches over to our table and stares vacantly at the group through a pair of thick glasses.

"Where's that American?" he finally garbles.

He wants our room key. He will also be known as "My Roommate."

As is often the case on trips of this nature, most of these people seem smart and funny, and as though the laughs come easily. This should be a great trip, except for that one guy.

The key still dangles from the keyhole when I climb the stairs to my hotel room. When the door opens, the air inside feels thick and musty, and I catch a whiff of something foul. An odor fills the room that was not there when I left for dinner, and it comes from him. In addition to his luggage, The Daft One has brought his own aroma to Africa: a pungent funk of sweat and old milk.

He is asleep in one of the twin beds, and I gag and breathe through my mouth while scrambling across the room to the open window. I press my face against the screen and hyperventilate the fresh air until I begin acclimating, then dive under the bed covers and pull a sheet over my nose. If his body odor is this offensive in a high-ceilinged hotel room with ventilation, inside a small tent it will be suffocating. I will have to sleep with my head out the door.

To compensate for smelling, The Daft One snores loudly. I wake up every half hour, convinced genetically altered, man-eating forest hogs are grunting next to my bed. After a few nights of this, oxygen and quiet will become endangered species and I will be sleep-deprived the entire trip. Then every creature in the kingdom—the lions and hyenas, the vultures and the dung beetles—will come en masse to silence the man and remove any trace of his tent mate.

DAY 3

Arusha, Tanzania

To ward off the symptoms of malaria, doctors recommend a weekly dosage of the prescription drug Larium for travelers before they even arrive in East Africa; I've been taking the pills for over a month now. They have a variety of pleasant side effects, including nausea, disorientation and hair loss. When you combine the drug with African beer, fine boxed wine and potent Zimbabwean ganja, you may experience technical difficulties that cause you to nearly stumble into a Zambezi campfire while dislodging quarters from your buttocks and into a cup in a bizarre game of Butt Darts—or so I vaguely seem to recall. Additional side effects include delusions, vivid hallucinations and what I'm experiencing now, a surreal nightmare.

In the nightmare, I'm asleep in a hotel room. Then a clammy, damp talon clutches my arm and presses against my hand. The fleshy claw nudges me again and continues until my eyes blink open. A figure hovers above me, silhouetted against the thin slats of light creeping between the window blinds. The creature is dripping-wet, flabby and gray. It is The Daft One holding a towel around his waist. Except this is not a dream. He is really standing next to my bed, half-naked, touching me. My eyes go wide, and I flinch into the mattress.

"I'm out of the shower, if you fancy taking one," he says.

Squinting at the travel alarm clock, I learn that it is only six o'clock in the morning. The group is not leaving for another three hours, so I don't fancy a shower just yet. I pull the covers over my head and contemplate a future sharing a small tent with this man. I weep quietly.

In the morning, we climb aboard the truck, stow our luggage and begin our inaugural game drive. The Bedford is our primary home and mode of locomotion for the next two weeks; some days we will spend more time aboard the truck than in our sleeping bags. The military transport vehicle of British origin is 10 years old, 25 feet long and has notched 600,000 miles. The truck is as sturdy as a rhino, taller than a giraffe and as subtle as a baboon's butt. It has more features and attachments than a knife from a neutral, alpine country.

A long, metal kitchen table unfolds from a slot in the back.

Nearly two dozen campfire chairs are crammed into a metal cubbyhole behind the passenger's door.

Pots and pans sit on a shelf that slides out from a locker.

Two half-doors fold down like attic staircases and turn into stepladders for climbing aboard.

A wide aisle bisects the truck and splits two facing rows of padlocked, cushioned seats.

A large wooden box filled with plates and silverware separates two smaller seats against the back wall.

Yard-long sections of cushions unlock to reveal individual cubbyholes for storing luggage and gear.

Sleeping bags, day packs and water bottles stow away on overhead shelves that wrap around the truck interior.

Compartments behind the seats hide food, books and kitchen supplies.

Maps and itineraries are taped to the front wall.

Panoramic windows are uncovered by all-weather tarps that are rolled up every morning and cinched off.

A small Pullman table folds down from the front wall and into the aisle for future card games.

Atop the cab, a single row of balcony seating is accessible by narrow metal ladders on each side.

A dozen tents fit inside the hutch in front of the balcony.

Firewood is cinched to a ledge in back, and 20 large water jugs are stored inside a space beneath the truck.

With all the gear strapped to it, the Bedford resembles *The Beverly Hillbillies* jalopy as it drives through the outskirts of town, past the La-Z-Boys, the stacks of two-by-fours and the bars, which are already busy at 9:00 A.M. Most of the roadside taverns are sponsored by Coke and Fanta. Each one shares an identical rectangular sign: two square soda logos flanking a name printed in the same boxy script you would find in a press-on typeface kit. The Simba Bar and The White House Bar are popular, but most impressive is The Swiss Bar and Car Wash, where a man can enjoy a Castle Lager while he gets his car cleaned.

The Bedford will need a good scrubbing after this drive. The paved road deteriorates the moment we turn off the main route, and by the time we reach the large coffee plantations that border the Arusha National Park, it is a brown dirt path with an unbroken hump of grass running down the middle. The truck slows after driving around a bend, and the guests reenact the scene from that dinosaur movie where the scientists see their first prehistoric creatures—except our group sees a giraffe, a very close giraffe. It is less than 25 feet from the Bedford and swivels a long neck around to watch us as the guests lunge for the right side of the truck.

"Giraffe," I say, establishing myself as The Guy Who Will Point Out Clearly Visible Animals.

The Bedford pulls over and two rows of travelers gather in the large window, clutching the railings and gaping at the giraffe in wide-eyed awe.

Everyone, that is, but The Daft One.

He remains on his cushioned seat and stares ahead blankly, seemingly unaware that he is in Africa and a live giraffe is outside the window. More giraffes stand behind the first one, and dozens of warthogs, impalas and Cape buffaloes nibble on the grass alongside them. Occasionally, they look up to see if the group is still watching and fumbling with cameras.

Marc videotapes the scene and narrates in French: "*Un plus de girafes de douzaine broute derrière le premier un et le Cap buffle et warthogs grignote sur l'herbe.*"

"There are zebras over there," I add, correctly identifying the distinctive black-and-white ruminants standing in an unobstructed clearing.

More than a hundred animals graze on a neatly eaten plain fenced in by a thick forest. The scene is Africa at its most idyllic, with nearly half a dozen species coexisting in peace and harmony.

"Now, if only a lion would run out and eat one like on *Big Cat Diary*. Then we'd have something," I say to mostly blank expressions. "What? Don't you guys have cable?"

The Bedford arrives at the park headquarters and maneuvers into a grassy lot with an adjacent picnic area. Arusha's most popular tourist attraction is relatively small, covering an area of just 53 square miles. This park is one of the few we are allowed to walk in, and a pair of uniformed rangers leads the group on a hike. Everyone, that is, but The Daft One, who stays behind while Juma and Thomas prepare lunch.

To make no mistake of their seriousness, the stern-looking rangers carry automatic rifles and wear crisp uniforms topped by natty green berets. They are twin Samuel L. Jacksons. Rule no. 1 of Safari, which was perfected on the Zambezi River while our armed guide led us through crocodile-infested waters in inflatable kayaks, is: Stay close to the man with the gun. Rule no. 1 is applied to Sam no. 2.

Flanked by the guides, the group heads down an embankment and into a damp meadow. We crisscross streams on wobbly log bridges and hike single file through knee-high grass to a wide plain. As compact as the park is, a different habitat appears in every direction. Acacia grasslands can be seen in the distance, a vine-draped jungle borders one side and the ragged profile of Mt. Meru rises over 15,000 feet behind a series of foothills.

The first thing I notice about the park, in addition to the variety of natural beauty, is the amount of exotic manure. Large bocce ball—size bombs stacked in crumbling pyramids dot the well-nibbled grass. The dung beetles are going to have a field day. Navigating this minefield is almost as treacherous as paddling around surly hippos, and we deftly skirt the toxic mounds on our approach to an enormous herd of Cape buffalo. The gregarious bulk grazers, whose crap this probably is, maintain guiltless expressions while they monitor our every move.

"Should we be this close?" Minouk asks me. "Do you think it's safe?"

"Stay close to the man with the gun," I advise.

Suddenly, QE2 slips on a rock and falls to the ground, a small bloody trickle marking the royal ankle. There is much concern, and the entire staff hustles to her side and lifts her to her feet. But QE2 is of hearty stock and dismisses the stumble as inconsequential. Later, Roy apprehends the loose rock and has it beheaded.

Before leaving the park and driving to our first campsite, Trevor, Brian, Judith and I scale the narrow metal ladders on either side of the truck and commandeer the balcony seating atop the Bedford's cab. The space is not uncomfortable, with a narrow, weathered cushion and a raised handrail to grip onto whenever the ride simulates a slow, lurching roller coaster. What the seats lack in legroom, they compensate for with a panoramic vantage point. We have bird's-eye views even of the birds and spy wildlife we might have missed sitting down below.

"Giraffes at nine o'clock," I say.

Through a break in the trees, half a dozen animals forage on a bushy hillside. The thick vegetation swallows the giraffe bodies whole so only their disembodied necks poke out of the flora. From a distance, they resemble carrot stalks in a bunch of broccoli.

"Monkeys straight ahead."

Wallenda-esque monkeys appear in front of us and tiptoe across a narrow branch as the truck bears down. A tree overhead appears to have been papered with black-and-white tissue, but the long, bushy tails belong to dozens of colobus monkeys that perch in the branches and nibble on the leaves.

Sitting in the balcony is not all monkeys and giraffes, though, and the ride demands constant vigilance. The truck is so high that we scrape the bottom of the canopy and have to dodge the low branches that hang over the road. The umbrella thorn and apple thorn trees are the worst offenders and bully us from above, threatening to rip our heads off with crooked boughs and sharp spikes. They are the kinds of sinister-looking trees that chase animated Disney heroines through forests. We are constantly hunkering behind the rail and shielding our eyes from the lethal two-inch-long nails.

"Go left! Go left!" we yell as the Bedford swerves around the meanest-looking ones.

Abruptly, a thorny talon reaches down from the trees. It snags my collar and grabs for my hat. A second wooden claw hooks me by the shirtsleeve and tries to snatch me out of the balcony.

In Africa, even the trees are carnivores.

Driving back into Arusha, the Bedford is its own parade. The large truck commands attention, and our elevated seating gives us the temporary sheen of celebrity. We are astronauts and athletes, and this is our dirty Fifth Avenue.

"Jambo! Jambo!" we shout.

The reaction is crazed. Children throw down their chores and slingshot out of thatched-hut homes. They rocket down dirt driveways and sprint along the roadside to catch up with the Bedford, as though it is the East African version of the ice cream truck. (Only a few of the children dispel the notion that they are just happy to see us by holding out their palms and yelling, "Money, money, money.") Women walking along the roadside with large bushels balanced improbably on their heads smile and wave. Men in roadside bars put down their Castle Lagers and acknowledge us with polite nods.

"Jambo! Jambo!"

We wave back with the enthusiasm of homecoming parade grand marshals and are giddy with cross-cultural affection. The effect of this frenzy is that by the time we reach town my grin is as big as a crocodile's, and you'd think I had gotten away with something. That's when the giant head of President Bill Clinton rises into the sky and blocks out the sun. His mug towers above the road and grins down from a billboard welcoming him to Tanzania from the week before.

"Jambo! Mr. President! *Jambo!"*

At our first campsite outside of Arusha, Kinyua makes a trip-altering announcement:

"If anyone wasn't happy about last night's sleeping arrangements," he says, "there are enough tents to go around so some of you can have your own. OK? All right."

The clouds part. A shaft of sunlight illuminates the tent pile in a golden glow. I clear-cut a path off the Bedford and launch unsuspecting British people out the open windows in a rush to claim a solo tent. I don't bother with the stairs but leap off the truck and hurdle to the tent pile in a single bound.

Just as the hungry lion will seek out a Thomson's gazelle with a sprained ankle, I separate a tent with a broken zipper from the tent herd and pounce. The canvas bag is clutched between tight jaws and its life is drained away. I drag the tent to a campsite and feast.

(Editor's note: This is a dramatization meant to underscore the author's enthusiasm at not having to share a tent with that one guy. No British people were harmed.)

"Let's see who knows everybody's name," says Kinyua, as the group gathers around the campfire. "Who wants to go first?"

Nobody wants to go first, but Trevor volunteers and begins naming the guests.

"Well, Brian's my mate. Tim and Janet. Steve . . . Roy . . . Roy's mum is Eliz—Evelyn. Judith. Scott, the Yank. Tony and Selena," he says.

He is doing well until he reaches the French-Canadian woman in the pith helmet and the wire-rimmed glasses.

"Veronica . . . Vicky . . ."

Valerie fumes politely as Trevor struggles to remember her name. He has the first initial correct.

"Vanna . . . Valentine . . . uh," says Trevor.

I have been thinking of mnemonics to help me remember names and avoid withering gazes such as Valerie's.

Trevor is missing a tooth. *T* for tooth, *T* for Trevor. One down.

Tim, conveniently, is slim. He is a Slim Tim.

Judith and her hometown, Sydney, have the letter *D* right in the middle of their names.

Tony, in a crisp, button-down oxford and khakis, is kind of . . . tony.

Brian is the guy who could convincingly play a mercenary. *Brian* and *mercenary* share *R* sounds and *N* sounds, proving just how far alliteration goes in remembering new names.

With his full beard, Roy reminds me of a monk or a friar. Friar Tuck is the most famous friar, from Robin Hood. Robin and Roy have the same first initials.

Susan and Sarah are introduced to me at the same time. That's a tough one: people you meet at the same time with similar-sounding names. Plus they are both tall—taller than I am—and have short hair. Susan is from Switzerland, and those both begin with *S* and end in *N*, almost. Susan, Switzerland. Sarah sounds like a proper British name.

When alliteration fails, celebrity similarity is a helpful fallback. Marc shares *M* initials with his follicle doppelgangers, Michael Stipe and Moby. Michael, Moby, Marc.

Selena has a more subtle shade of Christina Aguilera hair, a shapely figure and those sinewy arms. Plus they rhyme.

Kinyua will be called "Kenyahwu," "Kenwahyu," and "Kenwayahyah," and midway through the trip the group is still debating the proper pronunciation. His name is *Kin-you-wah*, I think.

Steve is The Daft One, and vice versa.

QE2 is obvious.

Coming up with hints for Janet proves impossible, so I have to learn it.

"It's Valerie," says Valerie.

Her name, I will remember.

Kinyua delivers The Tanzanian Explorer Orientation. We aim headlamps and flashlights at him to illuminate his speech, but he dismisses us with a bright flash of teeth.

"I will just smile and you will know that I am here," he says.

He describes our itinerary for the next two weeks. The Bedford will drive to Tarangire National Park tomorrow and camp near the park entrance. We will visit Lake Manyara and experience an authentic bush camp for a few days before heading into the Serengeti. The group will backtrack to Ngorongoro Crater and camp on the rim before finishing in the shadow of Mt. Kilimanjaro.

Kinyua explains what is involved in transporting a group this size across Tanzania and details the camp rules we need to follow in order to stay healthy, whether we're washing our hands or just the dishes.

"That's disinfectant over there," he says, pointing to a spray bottle that hangs from the Bedford's door. "After you go to the loo, spray your hands. OK? All right."

We learn which water jug to use for drinking and filling the plastic dishwashing bowls.

"The jug with the colored shoelace is the treated jug. So only fill your water bottles from here. OK? All right."

All the water on the trip is treated to eliminate any germs, particularly *Giardia lamblia*, a nasty parasite that comes from tainted, untreated drinking water. The infectious bug is a resilient microscopic cyst that causes intestinal distress of a brief duration, including nausea, diarrhea, abdominal cramps and low-grade fevers. The guides are diligent about treating the water, and the shoelace is moved from jug to jug, so we always know which one is safe.

"Here are your keys," Kinyua says, passing around leather string necklaces with small keys that provide access to the truck's padlocked cushioned seats and are worn throughout the trip.

We learn what goes where and who does what and what happens when. This trip is billed as a Limited Participation Camping Trip, which means we pitch in and don't pay nearly as much as the A&K guests. The guests help prepare meals, wash the dishes and do various camp chores. These tasks are the same ones you would normally do on an adventure trip, only now they are mandatory and scheduled.

"Scott, what would you like to do?" Kinyua asks me.

"What have you got?"

"You could load and unload the tents. They're in front of the balcony," Kinyua says, pointing to the top of the Bedford.

Hmm, that looks like a lot of work. At least a dozen large bags fill the space, and they are 20 feet off the ground.

"Someone needs to set up the chairs," he says.

Because Campfire Chair Storage sounds easy—Delusion no. 3—I volunteer to arrange the chairs at each new campsite and store them in their metal locker beneath the cab; Valerie is partnered with me.

Her boyfriend, Marc, and Tony are assigned to retrieve the tents from atop the truck, but Brian and Trevor usually toss them down because they ride in the balcony so often. Brian and Trevor also start the fire every morning and slide the kitchen table in and out of its slot.

At mealtimes, Tim and Janet wrangle on and off the truck the large wooden box that holds the dishes and silverware, while Judith and Sarah manage the plastic bowls used for washing dishes afterward.

A female quartet forms the Bedford Cleaning Committee, and they dust and sweep the truck every afternoon.

The Daft One and Roy are in charge of lugging the large water jugs back to the truck once they've been filled and treated by the guides.

As is often the case on trips of this nature, certain people make a larger contribution than others.

An attempt is made to engage The Daft One in a conversation. I feel a little guilty about opting for a single tent without any explanation but figure he is happier having his own tent, too.

"So Steve, is this your first trip to Africa?" I say.

"No," he says.

This is his fourth visit here, and Kruger National Park in the south is his favorite region. He was married once before and endears himself to the women by describing their gender as "very expensive creatures." (Trevor places a close second by wearing a "Ten Reasons Why Beer Is Better Than Women" T-shirt.) Talking with the guy is like pulling teeth, a procedure he appears well-acquainted with. A few people have better luck, and he occasionally amuses his countrymen aboard the Bedford with blustery outbursts.

In the evening, most of the group gathers at the campground's center, which has a restaurant, bar, self-service kitchen, showers and locker rooms. The rambling, stitched-together space looks exactly how a bar at a campground in Tanzania should look, with animal-print chairs and a sprawling thatched roof that forms peaks and valleys above our heads.

Our group takes over the zebra stools by the bar and we recap the day's sightings and exchange brief synopses of our lives:

Judith, the funky Aussie, is thinking about spending the winter in the Alps and working at a ski resort.

Tim tells me about his honeymoon, and how he and Janet were married during a stop in New Zealand on a monthlong, around-the-world trip that took them from England to South America to the South Pacific.

Janet and I trade advertising stories about our favorite commercials; she is a marketing professor and lectures to students and colleagues around the world.

Selena is a social worker with harrowing tales of working with families in distress, and Tony is studying for his MBA.

Sarah, the giggly blonde, is a math student between classes, living in London and looking for the answers in a safari.

Susan, the Swiss woman with the short brown hair, is a confectioner and makes gourmet chocolates in a small town outside Geneva.

Minouk is from the Netherlands and works as a general practitioner in Amsterdam.

Trevor manages a pub and Brian, who just tracked mountain gorillas in Uganda, enjoys having a pint there.

Marc and Valerie live in distant Canadian cities and have a long distance romance.

Roy works in video production, and QE2 recently knighted a Beatle.

By the end of the evening, we are getting along like old friends and the British are already making fun of me. When the group learns that Kentucky is my home state and I grew up in Atlanta, imminent mocking is on the horizon.

"You're from Jaw-juh?" Janet asks. "Well, fiddle-dee-dee."

Janet and Tony perform a variety of hick dialects of the great American South, dripping with "y'alls" and "honeys" and cornpone expressions.

"Y'all like to mix up a big batch of possum for supper?" says Janet. "Billy Bob, go kill us a possum."

"I will, after I marry my cousin," says Tony.

"Y'all like to marry your cousins, right, Scott?" asks Janet.

"Not as much as the royal family."

DAY 4

Arusha, Tanzania to Tarangire National Park

The trip routine is established the second morning. The local birds wake me around 6:30 A.M., and their exotic jabbering reminds me that this is Africa. After untangling myself from the sleeping bag, I fumble around the toiletry kit and start my day with an antibacterial wet nap with aloe. You learn pretty quickly to wash the face first, then the armpits and nether regions.

My shorts are zipped up, and the tent is unzipped for a weather report: It is already sunny and warm. I brush my teeth and spit the toothpaste residue out the tent door. I smell the pits of yesterday's T-shirt; it can be worn another day. I slap on deodorant and my favorite hat and make a brief sweep of the tent. My Tevas are Velcroed and I head to the campfire for coffee and a peanut butter and jelly sandwich on toast for breakfast. I chat with the other guests for a while before returning to the campsite to pack the tent.

The sleeping bag is stuffed into one gear sack; the sleeping pad is deflated and forced into another. My tent is emptied and the contents are packed away. The dew-covered tent fly is wrestled off the top and tossed over a tree branch to dry in the sun. The tent stakes are pulled up and slipped inside a bag. The tent is disassembled, and the poles, the stakes and the fly are wrapped into a tight, neat burrito and packed inside another bag. My gear is carried to the truck, and a sleeping bag, a water bottle, a backpack and a camera bag are stored in their assigned places. The guests navigate the crowded aisle and rummage through cubbyholes, putting away clothes and bumping into each other.

After stowing my gear, I gather campfire chairs and lean them against the truck's front left wheel. (Thomas takes over our storing duties today and makes the task look effortless.) The campsite is checked for stray clothes and leftover tent stakes, and we take our seats aboard the Bedford for the long drive—except for Minouk, who kneels in front of her cubbyhole for the next 20 minutes. Halfway to Tarangire National Park she is still rearranging her clothes or looking for something elusive. She reaches so far inside that the cushioned seat closes down on her haunches and only her lower body pokes out. The potholed road bounces the seat atop her thighs and for a moment it looks as though the cubbyhole is a giant, lip-smacking mouth and Minouk is being eaten alive.

In Africa, even the seats are carnivores.

Should the United Nations ever sponsor an International Waving Tour across Tanzania, our group would make worthy role models. The guests span the globe, and some of us are human metronomes. The waving is virtually nonstop as we attempt to greet every biped within 100 yards of the truck. You'd think we were seeing other humans for the first time.

"There's a kid over there," yells Janet, pointing toward a slim figure moving behind a patch of distant trees.

"*Jambo, jambo,*" we shout.

Many of the children who return our greetings and race barefoot after the truck make the international sign of the "waiter, check please." They clutch imaginary pens and write on invisible paper as they sprint behind us, scribbling in midair. The kids are trying to tell us that they would like a pen, a valuable commodity in these parts. No souvenir is quite as coveted as a pen from a foreign tourist; they are the autographed baseballs of the Serengeti. Kinyua explains the phenomenon this way:

"The kids see that you can afford to visit Tanzania. So, you are rich and successful. Rich people are smart. Smart people make good grades in school. So, if they use a smart person's pen, they will make good grades too."

"I pity the kid who gets Trevor's pens," says Brian.

To the kids, we are the Great White Gods of Writing Utensils, and surely we have come here to shower them with Bics. For the record, I have brought pens to Tanzania for this express purpose. A friend of mine visited Tanzania a few years ago, and when I asked for packing tips, she suggested taking along some pens.

"The kids love pens," she told me.

So, a box of a dozen ballpoint pens from the local Walgreens is added to my shopping list, along with miniature deodorants and blister remedies. The kids who get these pens will be the envy of their villages. They're brightly colored and sort of see-through and

51

futuristic, as if iMac made a pen. Currently, they are sealed in an envelope at the bottom of my duffel bag, locked away beneath the padlocked seat.

Whether 12 pens will be enough to make me a deity remains to be seen.

Kinyua drives the Bedford across the Ardai plains. Although Thomas is our designated driver, Kinyua spends most of his time behind the wheel. Thomas always sits in back with us and answers a barrage of tourist trivia.

"How long is a cheetah pregnant?"

"About three months," he says.

"What kind of tree is that?"

"Candelabra," he says. "The sap is poisonous."

"How do you say lion in Swahili?"

"*Simba.*"

"When are we gonna get there?"

"Not much longer," he says.

"You would kick ass on *Safari Jeopardy*," I tell him.

After a few hours of intermittent waving and quizzing, we arrive at our campground outside the gates of Tarangire National Park. A tall fence of slim trees with sharpened points hems in the acre-size outpost and keeps out the lions and hyenas, but not the fierce winds. They rear up the moment we disembark, and the group hunkers down to prevent our faces from being blasted by a howling wall of sand.

Bathrooms of questionable hygiene and weather-beaten chalets sit at either end of the campground, and a tiny bar is stashed in a corner. A few thatched-roof gazebos are sprinkled in between for dining and cooking, providing limited protection from the winds. Other than a few huts sitting across from the entrance of our isolated campsite, the horizon disappears in every direction uninterrupted by any man-made structure.

Local Maasai warriors have been hired as security guards at many campsites, and a few roam our desolate patch, armed with wooden staffs. They encourage us not to leave the campsite due to the local lion population, and we comply. Some Maasai are still fully nomadic, like the ones we saw driving in, and wander throughout the year with their cattle, searching for greener pastures. They have a mythical relationship with their livestock and believe their rain god granted all cattle to them for safekeeping when the earth and sky split. They claim that "reassigning" cows from other tribes is part of their covenant, despite the objections of the cows' original owners.

As they have for generations, some Maasai subsist almost entirely on their livestock, particularly a potent cocktail of cow blood and milk. They shoot an arrow into the jugular vein at close range, capture the spilled blood in a gourd and mix the concoction with milk. The wound is not fatal and is patched afterward, for refills. The cows are not only giant beverage dispensers, the Maasai turn fresh manure into cement for hut walls. Even the urine is collected for its medicinal properties and cleansing qualities. The Maasai are under increasing pressure to conform with a modern society, even though they have perfected the cow blood latte.

"We need flappers!" is a cry often heard after meals.

To save on paper towels and assure us of our environmental consciousness, we dry all the kitchen items by flapping them. To flap, you grab a plate or a bowl in one hand and a handful of forks in the other. Then you flap your arms up and down quickly, like an ostrich who dreams of flight. After every meal, we gather around the campfire and wave damp kitchen items in the air, making sure to avoid erratic flappers flapping sharp knives or the cheese grater. QE2, holding two large ladles, looks as though she's guiding a 747 to its gate at Heathrow.

"So have you been to the States before?" I ask Tony and Selena, while waving damp plates.

"We've been a few times, but never to Chicago," he says, turning two handfuls of forks into a pair of maracas.

"You guys should come visit," I say. "We'll have deep-dish pizza."

"Is Chicago famous for its pizza?" asks Selena, flapping two small bowls as though she's drying her nails.

"Yeah, deep-dish pizza. The Bulls. Chicago bang bang," I say.

"Chicago bang bang?" asks Selena.

"The mafia," I tell her, brandishing a couple of glasses and making machine gun noises.

DAY 5

Tarangire National Park

A peculiar cultural phenomenon unfolds on trips of this nature, wherein people who were complete strangers only days earlier now talk freely and openly about their most personal bodily functions. Rare is the visit to the loo that goes unreported, and campers query one another about the status of their toilet activity as casually as they might discuss the weather.

"Morning," a yawning Janet says as she approaches the breakfast table.

"Morning," I say.

"Good morning," says Selena. "Did you have a good night?"

"Tossed and turned a bit," says Janet while filling a mug with a steaming cup of coffee. "You?"

"Not so bad. Tony snored."

"Have you gone to the loo yet?"

"Yes. It was bloody awful."

"It was? Oh dear."

"It's filthy."

"Oh man," I say. "I opened the door and caught one whiff and didn't have to go anymore."

"Ewww," says Janet.

"It's Imodium perfume. And I was practically crowning."

"Imodium? What's Imodium?" asks Janet.

"It's like a cork in a pill."

"I hear they have pleasant loos at the park entrance," Selena says.

"Oh, that's lovely," answers Janet. "I think I might hold out."

"On the Zambezi my friend T.S. didn't go to the bathroom for five days," I tell the ladies while making a peanut butter and jelly sandwich on toast for breakfast.

"You're not going to put that rubbish in your mouth, are you?" asks Janet.

"Yes. It's the finest food known to man."

"That's almost more disgusting than the loo," says Selena.

"Peanut butter and jelly?"

Selena shudders.

"What? And you're having baked beans on toast?" I say.

"Baked beans on toast is a proper breakfast."

"So your friend," says Janet, "didn't he cramp up?"

"I don't know how he does it. He's like a camel."

"You'd think one of those big waves would squeeze it right out of him," says Selena.

This frankness is never more vocal than when the facilities are not what we're accustomed to, and more often than not, they're bloody awful. The raised flush-toilet technology, for example, is still just a glimmer in a Maasai eye in this corner of the world. You are more likely to encounter Elvis hitching a ride on a rare black rhino than visit the loo with your legs at a 90-degree angle above water.

The bathrooms at this particular campsite are dung saunas with oval holes carved in wooden floors. The cement-block closets have no ventilation, and the stalls feature gag-inducing, stench-scented deodorizers. The women quickly theorize that the toilets were designed by men with no working knowledge of the internal plumbing of the female form. The oval hole has a pair of angled bricks at one end, apparently for the feet. This awkward position, typically reserved for Romanian gymnasts and clumsy tortoises, restricts squatting and causes the women to pee outward, as though they are vying for their country's pride in a Urinary Olympics distance competition.

"How am I supposed to piss in that hole with those bloody bricks in the way?" Janet demands to know.

At any rate, the British women's team should take the gold out of sheer volume. In the campsite outside of Tarangire National Park, the prospect of more modern toilets at the park entrance elicits as much excitement from the group as the opportunity to see a large variety of wild animals up close.

The entrance to Tarangire National Park is not far from our campsite, and the Bedford arrives after a short drive. A small ranger station sits next to the road, and a metal gate separates two low brick walls crowned with sunbaked Cape buffalo skulls. An ornamental tree is welded into the gate, and the wrought iron figure mirrors the live tree rooted behind it. The first elephants of the trip forage next to the gate and are so still and quiet that at first glance they resemble a diorama from a natural history museum. I fail to point them out, thinking they could be giant promotional items. They look more like animatronic jungle-ride creations than real live elephants. Then a trunk moves. The leathery appendage is an exotic accordion, curling under with a handful of grass in its trunk. The elephants stand in a tight group, silent and massive, with arching, weathered tusks and acres of floppy gray ears. They are not more than 25 yards away and watch us with hooded, knowing eyes.

"Should we be this close?" Minouk asks me. "Do you think it's safe?"

"Always keep a slower and more delicious guest between you and the wildlife," I advise.

As is often the case on trips of this nature, I calculate how many of the other guests I can outrun and feel pretty safe. I could take QE2 and The Daft One in a footrace; Roy and Sarah look beatable too. Minouk has short legs. Trevor looks fast, and Tim and Marc appear athletic as well. In a dead sprint back to the Bedford, I would place myself comfortably in the middle. We inch closer until Kinyua says, "That's far enough. OK? All right."

Marc videotapes the scene and narrates in French: "*Nous sommes hors de Tarangire le parc national où une demie douzaine d'éléphants fourrage dans l'herbe.*" In French, it sounds as though the elephants are doing something complicated and remarkable, but really, they are just standing very still.

"How can you tell which elephants are the males?" asks Judith, one of the budding naturalists in our group.

The men wait for a punch line, but apparently she is unaware that the male elephant is gifted with a penis that scrapes the ground.

"The male elephant has five legs," says Marc.

Judith spends all day looking for the five-legged elephants.

Tarangire National Park is the Africa I have envisioned. The savanna stretches out as lazily as a yawning cheetah, gradually sloping upward. The light is spilled gold; the heavens are a new shade of blue. Huge piles of fluffy clouds are stacked atop one another, defying the sky to contain them. Overgrown origami umbrellas called acacia trees speckle the plains and stand alongside the ample-waisted baobabs, a tree house's dream home with a Medusa wig of thick, haunting branches.

Turn your head in any direction and choose among zebra, elephant, giraffe, warthog, baboon, Cape buffalo, wildebeest, ostrich and umpteen varieties of antelope. The group spends all day driving through the park looking for hot *Animal Planet* action, and I am kept busy pointing out clearly visible wildlife. Half a dozen giraffes lope between the trees in slow motion. The uninjured corpse of a zebra reveals the lucky animal that did not die of a lion bite. A rogue male elephant shakes his trunk at the Bedford in mock threat.

"That's a male," I say and nudge Judith until she acknowledges that now she is aware of the presence of a male elephant—thanks to my skillful tracking.

"There are wildebeests over there."

Near the end of the day, the Bedford heads toward the park exit and a sunset canvas of gold and purple brush strokes.

"Man, what a day. No crowds. Perfect weather. Flush toilets," I say. "But if only we had seen a lion. That would have made the day complete."

Then Trevor spots a lion.

A large male is not far from the road, neatly camouflaged in the tall grass. The lion does very little; in fact, he is not moving. He might even be asleep. In spite of his inactivity, the group cannot believe our good lion-hunting fortune. A sleeping lion! We are rapt. The Bedford is surely listing as everyone herds against one window, jostling for position and watching the slumbering cat.

Everyone, that is, but The Daft One.

He remains on the opposite side of the truck and appears unmoved by the proximity of a large carnivore. Suddenly, the King of the Jungle wakes, and we hold our collective breath. He throws back his mighty head, opens his tremendous jaws, bares his colossal incisors and unleashes a mighty . . . yawn. We are ecstatic about seeing The Great Yawning Lion. There is borderline mania at being this close to an actual sleepy lion. Out of nowhere, the savage beast flops his tail, perhaps to shoo away a pesky fly. The tail flops from one side of the massive carnivore over to the other, drawing an imaginary half circle in the air. The easily impressed tourists gasp in unison.

"He flopped his tail," someone whispers excitedly.

"That was lovely, wasn't it?"

"It went all the way over."

"I wonder if it will flop back?"

Tension builds as the group waits to see if the tail will flop back to its original position, but the lion leaves it in place. Still, we are beside ourselves. A yawning, tail-flopping lion! Never before has an animal doing so little brought such excitement to so many. He is doing next to nothing, and we are close to rapture. Every move or glance has us pointing and gasping for air. A blink of an eye thrills us; a clenched paw causes goose bumps. Without warning, the lion twitches an ear, his left ear. The furry tuft shivers on his head, flicking his golden mane out of the way. This is some substantial ear twitching—it wiggles for two or three seconds—and excited murmurs fill the Bedford. An ear-twitching lion! Abruptly, the male rises on his forelegs and stands up to his full height. Before we can even contemplate the magnitude of The Great Standing Lion, he starts to walk. Holy mother of God, a walking lion is not more than 25 yards away from us. The lion walks across the savanna, confident and indifferent, with decisive and evenly paced strides. Lion-induced euphoria erupts. Shutters click. Kodak stock skyrockets. People gape at one another in disbelief. A yawning, tail-flopping, ear-twitching, sitting-up, standing lion is currently *walking*. The massive cat is going somewhere, to do something, we speculate in hushed, earnest whispers. After covering 20 feet of grassy savanna, the King of the Jungle is worn out and lies down for a long nap. The group is tired too, and we collapse on the cushioned seats, winded and satisfied. Within a few minutes, we are already reminiscing.

"Remember when he yawned?"

"You could see his entire mouth."

"And when his ear twitched!"

"That was lovely, wasn't it?"

"It twitched for a while."

DAY 6

Tarangire National Park to Lake Manyara

In the morning, a few minutes after entering the Tarangire National Park, the Bedford comes across two male lions eating breakfast. They are having the dead Cape buffalo today, oblivious to the large truck parked nearby. The stationary vehicle alerts the other outfitters to something notable, and several smaller jeeps pull up to watch the carnage.

A jeep with an Abercrombie & Kent logo stenciled on the side pulls up and their guests poke their heads out of the sunroof. It's the cheese-and-grape-eating couple from the drive in from Nairobi, with the multicolored shorts and the ample waists, and they glare up at our elevated seating with a mixture of envy and travel-agent rage. None of the other tourists like us because we tower above them and always spot the wildlife first.

From the shade of a nearby tree, the two lionesses that probably made breakfast watch the males feast. The lions rip into the flesh and gnaw on a Flintstone-size slab of ribs. The hungry cats are ruthless and savage as they shred the large kill with their sharp incisors. The Cape buffalo has a gaping hole where his back should be, and one lion forces his head inside the body cavity. The buffalo's head and torso shudder, as if he is waking from a bad dream, but it is only the lion shoving his head around and tearing at the innards. He takes a large bite and emerges from the animal's backside with a bloody maw. All of a sudden, in the shade of the tree, the two lionesses begin to bathe and lick one another. The males stop eating. They stand up and watch the affectionate females.

"See? No matter the species, a guy will stop whatever he's doing to watch two females lick each other," I say.

"We are not so different, the lions and us," says Tony.

After the lion viewing, the Bedford returns to the campground, and we pack our gear for the drive to Lake Manyara. My legs poke halfway out the tent door as I fumble with a stubborn knot in one of the gear sacks. A shadowy figure appears in front of the tent and straddles my legs. The door flaps open and a long, dark arm reaches inside and grabs the bag out of my hands, like one of those miniature banks that snatches a penny. Peering out the tent door, I see a strange man standing over me and fiddling with the knot.

"Uh, hey buddy," I say.

I have not seen him in the guidebook before, but he appears to be some sort of Maasai Tent Warrior. Without asking, he grabs the sleeping bag out of the tent and stuffs the gear inside the sack.

"I can do that."

He tosses the sack aside, where it rolls into a low rock wall, and he disappears around the corner.

"What the hell," I say.

The tent begins to tremble and the fly is yanked off the top. The latches attaching the tent to the poles are unhooked, and it collapses around me.

"Buddy, I'm in here."

But my protests are as useless as my tent's busted zipper. The Maasai Tent Warrior is going to pack my tent and wants everything off the premises now.

"Dude, I can do this," I tell him as I crawl out of the tent, but get no response.

He slips the poles out of their holders and folds them quickly. He shakes my belongings out of the tent, which he lays atop the flap. He begins the burrito stage of the packing process, which involves rolling the tent, the fly, the poles and the stakes into one tightly proportioned package. He is packing the tent in record time, to be sure; no tent has ever been packed faster. He's rolling it wrong, though, so I'm reconsidering my tip options.

"You're doing it too big. It's not going to fit," I say, helpfully. "It needs to be longer. Yours is kind of stubby."

The tent is not going in. The Maasai Tent Warrior would have better luck coaxing a baby hippo in there. The ruckus alerts the other campers to the spectacle, and imminent mocking is on the horizon.

"Hey, why does Scott need help?" asks Trevor. "Why can't he pack up his own tent?"

"Those bloody Yanks, they can't do anything," Brian says.

"Late to every war," adds Trevor.

"Did you see what he had for breakfast?" asks Janet. "Peanut butter and jelly on toast."

On the surface, arranging the campfire chairs and storing them in a cubbyhole might seem to be the least demanding chore of the trip, hence my volunteering. The chairs are lightweight and fold easily; they should fit right in the metal locker beneath the truck's cab. But the task is difficult, and we have to attend a Campfire Chair Storage Seminar before we are even allowed to attempt it. It's complicated: Spatial relationships are involved; instructions have to be followed. The locker is a tight space and appears too small to hold the 22 chairs we're hauling across the country. This is a Rubik's cube of a puzzle where each chair has to be stacked facing a certain direction; the next chair has to alternate, and the one after that has to have the chair back facing up, and so on, before they will all fit.

"You have to put the first one in back-flap-side down. Turn the next chair the opposite way with the back-flap-side up," Kinyua explains. "Back-flap-side down, back-flap-side up. OK? All right."

Kinyua demonstrates the process by stacking half the chairs before turning the job over to us. Valerie takes charge and begins storing the chairs after I flip them in the proper direction. About the time the 18th chair goes in, the situation starts to look bleak and I wonder if the Maasai Tent Warrior is better suited for chairs. I push on the stack with all my weight to make more room while Valerie tries to squeeze in one more chair, but it is not going in. The North

American team cannot store the campfire chairs without foreign aid. We would have better luck coaxing a baby hippo in there.

En route to the park, Tim and I practice counting to 10 in Swahili.

"One is *mo-jaw*," says Tim.

"*Mo-jaw*," I repeat.

"Two is *mbee-lee*."

"*Mo-jaw. Mbee-lee*."

"Three is *ta-too*."

"*Mo-jaw, mbee-lee, ta-too*," I say. "*Ta-too*. Like the guy on *Fantasy Island*."

"Who?" says Tim.

Being the only American on the trip is a mixed blessing. I am something of a curiosity and am often required to speak on behalf of the entire nation on any given subject: colonial imperialism, *Melrose Place*, the merits of a peanut butter and jelly sandwich. As our country's sole representative, I have an obligation to portray us in the best light possible, avoiding any bad habits that might be attributed to The Ugly American. I never rush to the front of the dinner line or remind everyone how we saved their butts in World War II. Being a solid citizen is a priority, and I think I'm succeeding.

"Scott, you, we like," Janet assures me, after making fun of a loud American woman who pushes her way to the front of the postcard rack at a store on the way to Lake Manyara.

Of course, anything I do that is annoying, such as having someone else pack my tent or pointing out clearly visible animals, is also attributed to me being an American. I am OK with this arrangement. Plus I'm learning lots of British words. I *queue* up at the loo. *Fancy* this and that. *Cheers* means thanks. *Knarcky* is pissed. *Pissed* is drunk. *Porridge* is the same thing as oatmeal. Who knew? *Fanny* is vulgar slang for the distinguishing characteristic of the female anatomy. I learn this word the hard way.

"Where is my fanny pack?" I say one afternoon, as the Bedford drives across Tanzania. "Fanny pack, fanny pack, fanny pack."

Someone gasps. Selena clears her throat.

"What did you call that?" asks Janet.

"Scott—" says Tony.

"I'm sure I left my fanny pack up here," I continue, while digging through the backpacks and jackets on the overhead shelves.

"Scott—" interrupts Tony again.

"Hey, has anyone seen my fanny pack? It's green? Zips open?"

"Scott, don't say that," says Tony, as Selena shakes her head and QE2 turns a royal shade of red.

"Don't say what?"

"'Fanny pack,'" Tony mouths.

"'Fanny pack'? I can't say 'fanny pack'?"

"Stop saying that."

"What's wrong with 'fanny pack'?" I ask incredulously.

70

Tony whispers the answer to me.

"'Fanny pack'? I'm so sorry. It's such an innocent little word. Well, I guess Fannie Mae Candies isn't a big hit over in England."

"No," says Tony.

Tony is a willing conspirator for importable expressions, and I am often stopping conversations to jot down British slang to amuse my friends back home. *Bloody* is the most popular adjective among the English and can be used to emphasize just about anything, as in "You eat a lot of *bloody* peanut butter" or "What did that *bloody* Yank say now?" *Bugger* is another versatile word used to signify the Brit's disapproval of one thing or another. When QE2 finds a dirt clod on her crisp skirt, she exclaims "*bugger*" and swats it off. When Brian gives Trevor a randy *bollocking*—a severe reprimand—Trevor tells his mate to "*bugger* off."

Bollocks I heard years before, but Tony explains that the word is more versatile than the Sex Pistols pointed out. *Bollocks* by itself is sort of the universal expletive. If, during a game of spades, Selena bids zero and gets a trick, she will yell "*Bollocks!*" If Trevor is talking *bollocks,* he's talking nonsense. Adding the word *dog* to *bollocks*, as in "That's the *dog's bollocks*," transforms the phrase into something sensational, such as watching two lions shagging.

"So you just add the word *dogs* to *bollocks* and then it's something great?" I say.

"Yes, essentially," says Tony.

"How does that work?"

"Because a dog can lick his own *bollocks*."

71

The dog's bollocks is claimed as my trip catch phrase and I apply it to any appropriate situation, much to the amusement of the Brits.

"That was the dog's *bollocks*," I say in my flat, nondescript accent after an inspiring wildlife encounter or a particularly good dessert.

I've mispronounced the word the last 20 years, and Tony is determined to correct me before the end of the trip; it will take that long. To his chagrin, I pronounce the word "bull-ooks."

"It's ball-ox," he says. "Not bull-ooks."

Tony does not like the way I say "python" either.

"It's not Py-THAWN, it's Py-thun. Monty Py-thun. Why are you yelling the second syllable?" he asks.

"I'm not yelling it. That's how they said it on the show," I say. "Monty Py-THAWN'S Flying Circus."

"It's py-thun," Tony says. "Monty py-thun."

"Py-thun." I practice saying. "Monty py-thun."

My fake British accent is sprung on the group with the Tanzanian debut of The Hippo Safety Orientation routine from our recent river trip. I have been saving the tale, thinking the Brits might not find the humor in Americans faking British accents. This trip takes place during that whole Renee Zellwegger—playing—Bridget Jones nonsense, after all. The Hippo Safety Orientation's frequent imitation caused much laughter on the Zambezi River among the

Chicago Gang and was steadily parodied into legend. The part where Peter, the John Wayne/John Cleese combination, tells us what to do in case of a hippo attack is reenacted.

"Should your craft suddenly erupt three meters out of the water," I say in a clipped British accent, "you are not capsizing. You have encountered an angry hippo. Do not attempt to save your loved ones. Do not retrieve your sentimental college cap. Do not take this personally. The hippo is not angry at you. He is angry at your craft."

The Brits think my impersonation is pretty funny and retaliate with more takes on American dialects. Most of the Brits have the same opinion about Southern drawls as I do about their accents. Things are just funnier. Tony launches into a Bo and Luke Duke reenactment complete with appearances by Boss Hogg and Roscoe P. Coltrane. For a finale, he sings the entire *Dukes of Hazard* theme song.

"Just some good ol' boys, never meanin' no harm . . ."

Janet joins him in a duet.

"Beats all you ever saw, been in trouble with the law since the day they was born . . ."

Somehow, these two urban Brits know all the words to *The Dukes of Hazard* theme song. Hearing British people sing this in fake Southern accents while driving across Tanzania in a big truck is an unexpected trip highlight.

"Someday the mountain might get 'em but the law never will . . ."

Lake Manyara is a departure from the wide-screen vistas of Tarangire. The park is wedged in between the cliff walls of the Rift Valley Ridge and the 125-square-mile lake. The entry road seems to brush right up against the rust-colored escarpment and cuts through a narrow strip of jungle. We haven't driven 50 yards past the visitor's center before the Bedford is wrapped inside a leafy, green cave, with jutting branches for stalactites.

It is rush hour in the park, and a large clan of baboons sits in the road and limits our progress to a slow crawl. Dozens of smaller relatives fill the branches and perch on fallen tree trunks along the roadside, doing monkey things.

When Marc videotapes the scene and says, "*Ici nous sommes dans Manyara de Lac. Nous venons d'entrer le parc et est tombé sur les douzaines de singes qui asseyent par le bord de la route,*" it sounds as though the monkeys are being tender and romantic. But mostly, they just stick their butts in each other's faces, pick the fleas out and eat them. Some forage for grubs. One couple mates furiously. While sitting on the truck's comfortable cushions and enjoying the playful antics, I cannot help but envision a simian "It's a Small World" ride. Any moment now the monkeys will launch into a song that will stick with me all day.

The terrain changes every quarter mile as the jungle turns into groundwater forest, and acacia woodlands give way to the shores of Lake Manyara. According to the guidebook, the park is famous for a pride of tree-climbing lions, but Kinyua admits that this is false advertising and he has not seen arboreal felines in many years. He

74

does know where some cool lake-dwelling hippos live though, and he will drive us there instead, now.

The Bedford pulls up near a shore where a quartet of small geysers burst from the water. The hippos need to be photographed with a zoom lens right away, so Tony and I jump off the truck and run across the brittle, twisting branches with little regard to personal safety. A thick bog supports the tangled boughs, and it grows less thick and less supportive as we near the shore. We experience hippoxia: the state where one feels so confident he thinks he can run across a swamp and right up to a hippo and take its picture—Delusion no. 4. In no time, we are shin-deep in bog and our legs are speckled with mud. This is when the guides tell us not to go any farther.

"Stop! Stop! Come back! There are snakes over there!" they tell us now. They do not even mention the hippos.

En route to the park exit, the Bedford comes across a family of five elephants within trunk-swatting distance of the truck. The largest one is missing a tusk and is accompanied by a second adult, two juveniles and a baby no bigger than the truck's front tire. The elephants are having lunch next to the roadside and cast a wary eye as they vacuum the ground with their trunks. The scene could be from a theme park jungle ride—the animals are so close and lifelike—and the group quickly gathers on that side of the truck.

Everyone, that is, but The Daft One.

He sits on the other side, seemingly unaware that a family of elephants is right outside the window. Eventually, he snaps a single photo.

"You only need one," he says.

One of the juvenile elephants charges toward the Bedford and trumpets his long nose at us in mock threat, and the group jerks back in unison. His younger brother peeks from behind a small shrub and studies the older sibling. This one is impossibly small. He is the smallest elephant of the trip. In all of Africa. Ever. He could be a remote-control toy elephant, he is so preposterously cute and tiny. The group resembles a sitcom audience, sighing on cue as the little pachyderm imitates his big brother and tugs at small twigs. He attempts to pick up a loose branch with his baby elephant trunk, but it has a mind of its own. It curls upward and veers sideways, and he eyes the mini nose curiously. The group wants so badly for the little elephant to pick up the branch and hold it aloft that we become surrogate elephant parents, urging him on and whispering advice.

"The branch is too bloody big," says Janet. "He needs a smaller branch."

"He needs to push it against something," says Tony. "He's just pushing it around."

"He should push it against that little clump," I suggest.

Soon, our entire worldview, all our hopes and dreams, depends on whether the little elephant can pick up a stick. The elephant moves the loose branch across the dirt floor until it catches on a stump. He wraps the small tip of his nose around the stick and grabs hold.

"He's got it."

He coils his trunk around the branch and lifts it triumphantly in the air. The elephant is as surprised as we are; he cannot believe he lifted the stick. The group cheers, startling the little guy and causing the trunk to career out of control. The elephant watches in horror as the trunk zigzags in front of him and the stick pokes him in the eye.

The Bedford arrives at a campground not far from the entrance to Lake Manyara National Park, near the town of Mto Wa Nbu. The site is the size of a football field and resembles a well-tended forest, with a puzzle of freshly mowed lawns sectioned off by rock-bordered paths. Stubby wooden arrows bear names such as Mt. Kilimanjaro and Ngorongoro Crater and direct us to tree-lined campsites. Our tents pop up against one side of the campground, adjacent to a wall of tall hedges studded with flowering vines.

Next to the tents is a sprawling white house with a roof of brown peaks. High ceilings and hardwood floors enclose a lobby, several offices, a wooden bar and a large room with nap-inducing couches. An open-air gift shop sits next to the house, and several bungalows with simple furnishings form a corner at the opposite end of the campground. A cement-block building with showers and bathrooms provides the back wall for a long laundry basin with rusty spigots.

Most of the group gathers here to wash clothes, and local women wander over to tempt us with their cleaning services. My only dirty clothes are the ones I have on, so I get the bright idea that washing them in the shower will be easier than laundering the old-fashioned way. Feeling very efficient, I stand underneath the showerhead fully clothed, except for my shoes. The shower offers a brief spray that dies down to a trickle and stops before lathering can even begin. My plans foiled, I emerge from the shower in sopping wet clothes that are none the cleaner. I wash them the old-fashioned way and hang damp laundry on the sturdy communal clotheslines.

I relax on the lawn and digest another chapter of *Hannibal*. By now, the bad guys are training the monstrous forest hogs to appreciate the taste of human flesh by doing unspeakable things with live victims. A row of aluminum-stall gift shops sits across the street, and Janet persuades me to put down the book and check out the assorted souvenirs.

"Scott, do you need a pair of giraffe salad forks?" she asks.

"I think I can live without those."

"How about these?" she says, holding up a pair of carved elephant-head napkin holders.

"Can they cohabitate with the hippo plates?"

"This is you. Lion salt and pepper shakers."

"Small store, small prices," says the shopkeeper, who assures us he is our close, personal friend and has a special deal especially for us. He does not, however, have the lion salt and pepper shakers in a giraffe.

Back at camp, we toss a Frisbee around one of the open lawns and bounce a hacky sack off our knees. Tim befriends a local youth and kicks a soccer ball with him and Marc. I befriend a local bartender and have a few beers with Trevor and Brian. The group enjoys a relaxed, carefree afternoon, our last one.

After dinner, the thrice-daily flapping routine continues. We spend almost an hour of each day flapping, about 20 minutes per meal—more for dinner, less for lunch. The group stands on the lawn and forms an atypical aerobics class, as a dozen people line up in three rows, holding kitchen items and waving them in the air.

"Be sure to stretch out before drying the big pot," I say to Tony.

"Right, I wouldn't want to pull a muscle."

"We're going to be in great shape by the end of this trip," says Selena.

"Yeah. We should make a flapping fitness video," I say.

"That would sweep the country," says Tony. "People love to work out with their dishes."

By now, theories are hatched that a comprehensive, full-body regimen of cardio-conditioning and muscle toning can be achieved by flapping.

"The plates create their own resistance and tension, see? Now, if you do this," I say, swinging my arms across my chest, "you'll target the pecs."

"Scott, that is quite a fashion statement," says Tony, flapping the dishes over his head.

"What is?"

"The socks-and-sandals combo," he says, referring to the fact that I am wearing a pair of light fleece socks with my Tevas.

"Socks and sandals?" I say, flapping behind my back and how famous guitar players might flap.

"Yes, it's fascinating."

"You've never seen people wear socks and sandals?"

"In Miami once, but the guy was 80," Tony says.

"These aren't dress socks," I say, clanging my plates together like giant cymbals.

"I've just never seen that combination before and wondered if you invented it."

"Yeah. I get a royalty. Bend the elbow a little more, Selena. There you go," I say.

"Peanut butter and jelly, socks and sandals. You're just very adventurous," says Tony.

After flapping, we gather outside of the main house and sit on the lawn, drinking and discussing our Bics. Many of the guests heard the same advice my friend gave me and brought along pens for the local children. Some people are giving their pens away as we travel through the countryside and tossing them from the truck whenever we pass a group of kids. Other guests are holding on to their pens until the end of the trip when the Bedford reaches Kilimanjaro. Our outfitter supports a local school there, and Kinyua encourages us to save our pens until then.

"That way the kids that get the pens, you know they're in school," he says.

In Tanzania, the children only attend school if their parents can afford tuition, and this is a poor country.

"If a kid is hanging out on the roadside he probably doesn't even go to school. He doesn't have paper. What does he need a pen for?"

The guests split into two camps: the pro-tossers and the anti-tossers. Some people prefer the instant gratification of giving a pen to a kid who sprints a hundred yards after the truck. They want to see where their pen is going.

"If a kid runs a hundred yards, he's getting a pen," Valerie says. "Besides, it's nice for a poor kid to get a pen. They have so little. The least we can do is give them a pen."

I was unaware that giving my pens away would require a moral decision, but tossing them from the truck seems a little distasteful, especially when there are more kids than pens and they start punching each other. It seems to further the notion that white people drive around by the truckload tossing pens to little African children.

"Turns the blokes into little hooligans," says Brian.

This divides The Great White Gods of Writing Utensils, and we debate the issue over Castle Lagers late into the night.

DAY 7

Lake Manyara to the Mangola Bush Camp

On the first few mornings here, my alarm clock is a jarring riot of birdcalls. The "du-duddly, du-duddly" of the black-collared barbet. The "wee-wee diddly" of the paradise flycatcher. The "tchi-tchi-trrrrrrr" of the rattling cisticola. Around 5:00 A.M., I am rousted by a heretofore-silent species, The Hurling Camper. The elusive creature sounds like this: a hurried, frantic "zip" (the sound of the tent doors being unzipped as fast as humanly possible), followed by a prolonged, painful "hurl" (the sound of prolonged, painful hurling). The call is an urgent one and comes from the tent next door. As is often the case in the animal kingdom, a second Hurling Camper soon answers the first one.

"Ziiip, huurrl," it sings. "Ziiip, huurrl."

A third Hurling Camper chimes in from across the way, and soon the entire campground is a gaggle of zipping and hurling. A passerby might conclude that our campground is a Hurling Camper sanctuary for the density of the species in this small area.

An hour or so later, upon opening the tent flaps, I am greeted by the singular vision of Sarah, whose tent sits across from mine. Only her disembodied head is visible, and it pokes out from the bottom of her tent door. For a moment, she resembles something between a Larium dream and a Lewis Carroll hallucination: a tortoise-shaped creature with the tiny head of a blonde woman and the body of a giant domed tent. Then she hurls.

Overnight, more than half the group has been stricken with a nasty bout of nausea and dysentery. Nine out of the 16 guests are sick. Selena, Tim, Janet, Susan, Sarah, Minouk, Marc, Valerie and Roy spend the early morning purging from either end and exchanging feeble greetings en route to the loo. They gather around the campfire and stare cheerlessly at breakfast offerings they can't keep down; their tents are packed in slow motion. I retrieve a packet of Pepto-Bismol chewable caplets from my toiletry kit and wander among the wounded, offering medication. Most of the Brits are unfamiliar with the pink remedy, so my advertising background takes over.

"Pepto-Bismol? Well, it coats the stomach and provides relief from nausea and diarrhea in no time at all," I promise.

To add to the unpleasantness, today's drive is the most brutal one of the trip. The group endures a five-hour ride on a stormy sea of dirt road into the middle of nowhere, which is Mangola, near the Kideroo Mountains. Salt spray is replaced by blowing dust, the waves by Bedford-swallowing potholes that toss us about the truck. This is a once-in-a-lifetime confluence of bumpy, unpaved road, skin-scraping sandstorms and the constant threat of impromptu hurling and emergency stops. Occasionally, a guest has to dig a latrine behind the most discreet shrubbery.

The slow-motion roller-coaster ride is a lurching, agonizing crawl. Every trough is magnified; every gully has us listing to and fro. People are miserable, strewn about the Bedford, searching for positions that provide some degree of comfort. Valerie collapses into a front corner as Marc curls into the fetal position and buries his head in her lap. Roy takes the opposite side and turns the vibrating interior wall into a pillow. Sarah, one of the worst, is obliged a long stretch of seat cushion. Selena folds a jacket over her arms and buries her head in the fleece. Janet clutches one of the window railings and holds on defiantly.

Occasionally, a passenger hurls over the side. The sick guests do not even bother to signal Kinyua with the Bedford's emergency alarm button (that's two beeps to stop; one continuous beep to stop *now*). They just lean their heads out the open windows as the truck drives along and empty their stomachs on the parched dirt roads. Fortunately, only the people sitting in the very back resort to this.

It gets worse.

Our drive turns into a theme-park ride gone awry when an army of whistling thorn trees attacks the Bedford. The trees line a narrow road and resemble a gauntlet of barbaric medieval weapons with crooked branches and dozens of long, sharp thorns. The truck brushes against the supple boughs and pushes them forward to the breaking point, until they snap into the truck interior where sick people are resting their heads by the open windows. The dreaded branches are as lethal as nail-spiked whips, and they launch inside the truck with the tenacity of well-armed mosquitoes. We leap up at the last second to swat them away from ailing guests, but the sharp spikes tear at our clothes and slash our arms and faces.

To pick up the slack of our fallen comrades and keep morale high, QE2 and I wave dutifully to the families who live along the roadside. Our animated, cheerful waving stands in stark contrast to the ailing group scattered lifelessly about the truck, but there are indications that this woman might not be the real QE2. She waves with adolescent enthusiasm, unlike the parade videos you always see of her where she is stiff-armed and deliberate and just rotates her arm as though she's screwing in a light bulb. This woman really waves, and the kids catapult out of homes hundreds of yards away and sprint down dirt paths, scribbling in midair. In the balcony, Judith encourages the kids toward the truck with a frenzied, two-handed, over-the-head maneuver, as though she's signaling for help; the sun projects her waving silhouette against the countryside as the Bedford drives across Tanzania.

"This would explain why the East African sprinters always did so well at the Olympics," I say to Tony. "They grow up running after tourists who might have a pen."

"You've given this some thought, have you?" says Tony.

"You run a 100-yard dash every time you see a truck? You're getting the gold."

The Bedford's emergency alarm interrupts us. Somebody wants off the truck; they want off *now*. We come to a hurried stop, and Marc walks to the back of the vehicle and leans out an open window. This is a good group to be sick in front of, and there is no shame here. But imagine the children's great shock and horror when they discover the Great White Gods of Writing Utensils are not tossing their pens today. They are tossing their cookies.

The Bedford climbs the Rift Valley Escarpment for eye-stretching views of Lake Manyara. The valley ridge resembles an 8,000-mile-long pair of nutcrackers, reaching from Turkey to Mozambique. The eastern arm of the rift valley ridge cuts a ragged profile along the shoreline and appears to slide into the lake. At one scenic overlook, I offer to take QE2's photo.

"Oh no, dear. There shan't be any photos of me," she says, patting my forearm warmly.

During a prolonged stop at a T-shirt shop with an elevated flush toilet, the truck parks across the street from a mud-walled, thatched-roof home. A few adults lean against the front of the house, while half a dozen children sit next to the road. Unlike most of the kids we've seen on this trip, they do not run for the truck or beg for handouts; they sit quietly and watch us in colorful, mismatched clothes, mostly extra-large sweaters with shorts. QE2 takes this extended break to indulge in an act of international goodwill.

"Oh, I must hand out a few pens," she says, rummaging through her purse as though looking for a tissue.

She collects a handful of pens, climbs off the truck and walks toward the children. They watch her approach and gravitate around her as they might a favorite grandmother, feeling the fabric of her skirt, touching a hand. QE2 does not toss the pens; she bequeaths

87

them to each child, one at a time, without any punching or tackling. As befits her royal personage, this is a proper and refined giving of the pens. It is a little graduation ceremony right here in the middle of Tanzania. QE2 reconsiders her photo decree and gathers the children around her for a portrait. She adjusts them as expertly as a homeroom teacher, brushing dirt off a young boy's sweater and spinning their faces around toward the camera. Nobody can take their eyes off her.

The road to Mangola is a thirsty track, and the Bedford kicks up a steady cloud of dust. To keep our noses from forming dirt landfills, Tony and I sport bandannas over the lower halves of our faces. In my weekend safari garb and Tony's crisp oxford, we resemble the most nonthreatening bank robbers ever outfitted by North Face and J. Crew. Nobody else takes the simple precaution, which is a solid deterrent against the thick and choking dust.

The bandannas come in particularly handy when Killer Wind Spout Pt. II debuts: A Bedford-seeking cyclone takes shape nearby and chases us across the dry plains. The twister begins life with the heft of a Roman column, and by the time it attacks the truck it is as big around as a baobab. Kinyua parks across from a small tree that trembles in the spout's wake and barely shelters a hapless Maasai man who flattens himself on the ground. The cyclone pauses above the man, tearing at his blanket and shrouding him in a gritty cloud. He may be a warrior, but his thin *shula* offers little protection against this Tanzanian devil. Resembling a scene from an alien abduction movie, the portal spins furiously around the Maasai and tries to levitate him. The force is not strong enough to lift the man into any spaceship, but the spout gives him a thorough dirt whipping before turning on us. The Bedford is on a collision course with the twister, an iceberg to our Titanic. Here it comes, hurtling toward the truck with the fury of an aggravated rhino. We grab window railings and brace for impact, wide-eyed and anxious about this new animal encounter.

The spout wraps the Bedford in the middle of a thick haze and visibility drops to five feet. The grainy swirl holds us in her midst, and we view the world through whirling brown glasses. The circular motion gives the impression that the Bedford is falling down a long helix, spiraling into the land that time forgot. I keep expecting a wildebeest to fly by or a witch riding a bike, but our view is only a 360-degree curtain of spinning dirt. Abruptly, the wind changes direction and the twister passes through us like a dirty ghost. It leaves a souvenir: a fine sheet of earth that covers our faces, our clothes and every surface of the truck interior.

The Bedford arrives at our destination: an authentic bush camp. No bathrooms, no gift shops, no fences; just a grassy field tucked away at the end of a canopied dirt road and ringed by a forest full of monkeys. The campground is crowded with tents; an earlier group has already staked out the premium sites. After five hours of driving down the most isolated, unwelcoming roads in Tanzania, barely seeing another vehicle, we arrive at Woodstock. The Bedford navigates around the smaller vehicles and claims the less desirable end of the meadow, where it becomes swampy and begins to slope.

It is all the sick kids can do to grab their sleeping pads, stumble out of the Bedford and collapse in the shade, where they will remain for the next few hours. Trevor and Brian spearhead a move for the healthy guests to assemble the sick people's tents, while Thomas cleans hurl tracks off the side of the truck with a sturdy wire brush. The camp resembles a mobile army hospital, with inert casualties scattered about a bivouac of green tents.

Tim approaches me on my way to the campfire. He comes to an abrupt stop a few feet away and places his hands over his midsection. Then he kneels on the grass and quietly empties his stomach. Even while hurling, the Brits maintain a certain level of civility and refinement.

The short-drop toilet is a communal waste storage system typically employed in authentic bush camps. The system is perhaps better known by its more common name, "the hole." Kinyua, Trevor and Brian dig our hole at the furthest end of the grassy meadow, around the corner from the campsite. The facility is tucked away behind a junkyard of brush and fallen tree trunks, but it is far from private.

The hole is two feet long, a foot and a half wide, and I pray never to learn how deep. The unruly shape requires the dexterity and alertness of a splayed-out giraffe trying to snatch a drink from a crocodile-infested watering hole. Under the best of circumstances, this is no place for tea. When a dozen people are experiencing simultaneous intestinal distress, the locale is best left unimagined.

The hole requires its own Bush Camp Hole Orientation. To maintain some decorum, Kinyua teaches us the Empty Soda Can on a Tree Branch System to indicate loo occupancy. A thin sapling with a few spindly branches stands alongside the path to the hole, and an empty aluminum Coca-Cola can and a garden spade sit nearby.

"When you go to the hole, stick the can on the tree branch. Take the spade with you and after you go, throw some dirt in there," he says. "Then bring the spade back to the tree and take the can off the branch, OK? All right."

It sounds simple enough, but it is not long before The Daft One incites loo anarchy by failing to remove the soda can and taking the spade with him to his tent for some unspecified digging.

After tracking down the garden spade, Janet begins to play culinary detective.

"What made so many people sick at the same time?" she wonders.

What did the sick people eat that the healthy people did not, or so the reasoning goes. Our dining history is retraced: Beef over rice, the last supper before the deluge, becomes Public Enemy no. 1. Enough witnesses testified that the meal did not agree with them going down, much less coming up.

"It was a little tough, but I ate it and feel great," I say. "I mean, I feel OK."

Yesterday's lunch is scrutinized, and a particular salad is tried but not convicted. Somehow, the culprit is narrowed down to the mango fruit plate from our lunch at the Tarangire campsite.

"Who had the mango fruit plate for lunch when we were at Tarangire?" asks Janet. "Scott, did you eat the mango?"

"I didn't eat the mango," I say.

Improbably, none of the healthy guests—Tony, Brian, Trevor, Judith, QE2, The Daft One or I—ate the mango.

"It must be the mango," Janet deduces.

Solved: It's Colonel Mango in the Tarangire camp with the fruit salad.

In the late afternoon, a small group visits a nearby freshwater spring to swim, bathe and do laundry. This is a potentially hazardous move and frowned upon by most outdoor magazines.

"There Could Be Dangerous Animal Crap in That Water!" the headlines scream.

But Kinyua gives us his blessing, so Brian, Trevor and I place our personal hygiene above common sense. Judith and Susan have good intentions of bathing and washing clothes as well, but upon seeing the naked male locals splashing in the stream, they remain discreetly on the banks and ponder their *Playgirl* letters.

Freshly scrubbed and laundered, I head to the campfire for pre-dinner cocktails. Only five guests are healthy enough to enjoy Juma's cooking tonight, and the flapping is easy. Juma is quieter than usual and may carry an extra burden: that some guests hold him responsible for feeding them bad mango. A few people have shown signs of life, but for most, the day's highlight is moving their sleeping pad from outside on the grass to inside a tent. In the evening, a rumbling of concern for The Daft One wafts through camp.

"Have you noticed Steve acting strangely?" Tony asks me.

"You're kidding, right?"

"He's just sort of sitting there. He can't answer questions. I don't think he knows where he is."

"And that's different how?"

Big surprise here: The Daft One is showing signs of daftness. He appears to be suffering from something that does not involve nausea or diarrhea but equilibrium. While sitting in his campfire chair, he slowly tips over to one side and tumbles to the ground. Climbing down from the Bedford, he misses a step and tumbles to the ground. He appears delirious. He wanders aimlessly and blabbers incoherently.

There is much concern.

I consider telling the group that this is not entirely new behavior, but instead Tony and I herd him to his campsite, using our flashlight beams as border collies, and help him inside his tent. Later, someone suggests that we should check in on him to make sure he hasn't tumbled out of his tent. Kinyua thinks this is a good idea. One of the guests, perhaps.

"What about Minouk? She's a doctor," says Kinyua.

And so Minouk unanimously wins the title of The Daft One's personal physician.

"What's wrong with him?" she asks.

"Well, he's been tipping over," I say.

"He's tipping over?" she asks.

"He fell off the truck. He fell out of his chair."

"Oh no."

"He wanders around. He's sort of delirious," says Tony.

"Ewww," says Minouk, the doctor, and we wonder if she makes that face with all her patients.

"Not much of a comfort, I'd imagine," says Janet.

Susan accompanies Minouk as she weaves between the tents to The Daft One's, and when she asks him how he's feeling, he becomes belligerent and accuses Minouk of plotting to send him to a hospital. Her prognosis is to leave him alone and see how he feels in the morning.

Meanwhile, Susan discloses that she has taken a baker's dozen Imodium in the space of a day, quadruple the recommended dosage. She will not visit the hole ever again.

DAY 8

Mangola Bush Camp

I wake up early to see if any monkeys have stolen my laundry from the branches of the umbrella thorn tree overhead. The tent is unzipped, and the door flap droops over like a heavily jeweled Maasai ear. Silhouetted against the morning light is the rolling mass of The Daft One, whose nylon dwelling sits a few feet across from mine. My day begins with the image of him standing in the doorway of his tent, naked, a sleeping bag clutched around his waist. This is the second time he has been silhouetted naked in front of me before breakfast, and that was not in the brochure. He is waiting for me.

"I've had a bit of an accident in the night," he says. "Could you be a good chap and fetch me some fresh trousers and a towel from the truck?"

My mouth makes the shape of an *o*. An accident? What kind of accident can you have in a tent? Did he tumble off his sleeping pad and plummet to the tent floor? This does not sound good. I slip on some shoes and hurry to the Bedford to fetch the man some clean clothes. Brian and Trevor are already up starting the fire, and we rouse Juma to unlock the truck. I try to remember which cubbyhole is his and sniff out The Daft One's duffel bag on the first try.

"He said he'd had an accident. Wanted me to bring him some clean clothes," I say while rummaging through his stuff. "He was standing in his tent when I woke up."

"He was standing in his tent when I got up," Brian says. "And that was half an hour ago. I waved to him, but he just stared ahead."

Trevor visits a nearby spring and fills a bowl of water for him. When I deliver his clean clothes, The Daft One warns me not to come too close.

"It's a bit smelly," he says. Then, "You're a fine chap."

I pull my laundry off the umbrella thorn tree, whose sturdy spikes make reliable clothespins, and climb inside the tent, the incredible solo tent. My sleeping bag is a welcome refuge from the not so distant sound of a nearby tent being scrubbed.

Meanwhile, I am a fine chap.

This part of the itinerary is scheduled for a series of cultural encounters before the big-game events of Ngorongoro Crater and the Serengeti plains. The original plan was to submerge the group into a real-life bush camp and visit indigenous tribes, not for us to hurl a trail across Africa. Some of the sickest guests prove to be the sturdiest troopers, however, and will not let a little intestinal distress and low-grade fevers interfere with their holiday enjoyment. Roy, Sarah, Marc, Valerie and Minouk join the healthy guests aboard the Bedford.

The first native people we visit are called the *Hadzabe*, which sounds like Japanese horseradish. The truck drops us off on a barren plateau a mile from the tribe's homestead, and we hike across a pockmarked stretch of dusty scrub brush. A downhill maze of gnarled branches and barbed shrubs funnels us onto a plain, and a portable village appears in a clearing. On a patch of stubbly earth, half a dozen thicket igloos are tucked among the shadiest trees, and a family of nearly a dozen—including several adults, a range of children and a baby no more than a few months old—is introduced to us. The tribe members are traditional hunter-gatherers and live as they have for thousands of years, relocating every few days and subsisting on whatever they can hunt and/or gather, without growing crops or raising livestock.

They dress in ornate necklaces of beads, well-worn Abercrombie & Fitch cutoffs and animal pelts. One of the men dons a fresh pelt as a vest. The garment is an entire small cat, complete with the head, and he drapes it over his shoulders and across his chest, using the incisors as a clasp. The bows and arrows the man displays are beautifully crafted and studded with feathery tufts. The tribe also has a few water jugs, blankets and rock tools among their possessions, and that's about it. They return to their normal lifestyle while we are invited to take photos and look inside see-through huts. No matter where in the small camp I go, the eyes of the dead-cat vest follow me.

One tribe member hunches over a stone workbench and sharpens an arrowhead with a small rock. A stoic mother nurses an infant on a woven mat with two older children. The difference in lifestyles is slightly awkward and fascinating, and a camera hangs from my shoulder with an expensive weight. As part of our complete adventure package, the man in the dead-cat vest teaches the tourists how to start a fire with a stick. A few guests take turns rubbing the long, finger-thick branch between their palms as it balances on a bed of kindling and a flat stone, but the intense friction quickly burns the white man's soft hands, and we are unable to start a fire in the bush.

The two elders lead us on a hunt, and we follow them into the dry brush, crawling through thick vegetation and beneath snaking vines. They peer around bushes and study the ground for animal tracks, arched bows and poisoned arrows at the ready. Sadly, there are no animals here. They have all been alerted by the sound of a dozen tourists tromping through the trees and bushes, chatting and cursing the prickly vines. The hunters come to an abrupt stop and kneel on the ground. Do they hear something? They confer in hushed whispers and appear to formulate a plan. Something important is about to happen; everyone can sense it. Our cameras are poised and our lenses are ready to zoom. Is there prey nearby? One man places a palm flat on the ground as though sensing an antelope's movement.

Aha, he seems to be thinking. It is the sprightly one with the torn tail, who favors her left leg.

The other man breaks off a section of branch and stands the long twig upright atop a flat rock. He rubs it between his palms and starts a fire with the stick. The man in the dead-cat vest pulls out a hand-carved wooden pipe and lights it with a handful of kindling. The hunters are not hunting but have stopped for a smoke. One hunter inhales deeply from the pipe and coughs for nearly a minute. This is a foul thing, it would seem, but the other guy wants a hit too. Their smoke break ends, and the hunt resumes.

Up ahead, the hunters track what can only be a hearing-impaired dikdik that has not been alerted by our elephantine approach. Proving natural selection, the nervous dikdik is caught in one of the hunter's sights. The slow, loping arrow finds its mark 15 yards away from the intended target and lands softly in a shrub. Finally sensing danger, the dikdik pops up and disappears into the bush.

When in Tanzania, 'the dikdik pops up and disappears into the bush' does not sound like Swahili for shagging.

During the hike in to meet the Hadzabe, I start to not feel so good. And not just about the tribe having to move all the time—which is such a hassle—but as though I'm going to hurl. A sudden queasiness fills my stomach, and the taint of bile creeps up my throat. The bullet has not been dodged; worse, I have blown The Mango Theory.

Whenever nausea looms, my body notifies me by producing unimaginable quantities of saliva. I am a spring. Something alien resides within me, so my glands inundate my belly with enough spittle to cajole my body into expelling the nasty bits. There is an urgent concern that I might hurl right here, where this tribe of indigenous people has welcomed us into their simple world.

I have been sick in some interesting places before—airplanes, buses, Costa Rica—but this would merit a certain amount of distinction: to fly halfway around the world to Africa, visit a tribe of hunter-gatherers and throw up in their front yard. The reputation of The Ugly American would certainly be sealed here. The tribe would have to move too. They're going to move anyway; that's what they do. But they'd have to relocate sooner if I ralphed on one of the huts, and I would feel horrible about it.

So instead of obliging my body, I spit repeatedly. Gobs. I am an automatic sprinkler, irrigating the parched countryside and marking every fifth step with a saliva trail that leads from hut to hut and deep into dikdik country. They are too polite to say anything, but the Hadzabe would no doubt prefer that I throw up on a hut if I would just stop spitting everywhere.

Our morning with the Hadzabe ends mercifully, and we say goodbye. A few people leave T-shirts and shorts with tribe members; Tony gives the leader a handful of shillings for a future shopping spree. I lumber across the plains and begin the slow ascent up the steep maze, ducking around bushes and swatting away thorny branches. We hike across the parched scrub brush to the Bedford, and I take a precautionary seat in the very back. On the drive to our campsite, I cease the spit decision and await fate. I must not look very healthy, because back at camp my listless demeanor and deliberate pacing prompts Valerie to ask how I'm doing.

"I'm gonna be sick soon," I say.

She offers me a sympathetic smile and welcomes me to her increasingly less exclusive club.

"Vomiting is demanding work," she says.

The end comes quickly. A rumbling begins in the cellar of my stomach and a churning swell floods my gut. I hurry toward the perimeter of the campground and seek out a nice spot. The Woodstock campers have left, so my options have practically doubled, although it would have been satisfying to hurl on one of their tents—they kept peeing right behind our kitchen table. My pace quickens as a wave strains for an exit, and I speed-walk toward a secluded plot of grass in the embrace of a shady sycamore fig. Hunched over, under the noonday sun and the watchful eyes of a family of curious baboons, near the end of a canopied road at a bush camp in wildest Tanzania, I return the contents of my stomach to the African soil in the great circle of life.

I do my best Victoria Falls impersonation, and a thick, muddy torrent gushes from my contorted figure. My stomach makes a fist, and a painful deluge spews forth, ejecting a bellyful of wrath and bile. It is beyond the realm of human endurance that my body can hold this much, but every time my gut feels empty, it clenches and unleashes another racking wave. I am a human fire hydrant, flooding the grassy meadow on a sunny afternoon. My repetitive hurling is so resonant and violent that a flock of startled birds flees a nearby treetop, and the baboons take defensive positions in the higher branches. Finally, my stomach runs dry and I drop to my knees before the soiled grass, hacking and spitting. Tony and Brian lead the charge to see if an alien has burst out of my stomach, and there is much concern.

"Nothing more to see here," I mumble.

Vomiting *is* demanding work. I will barely move and not eat for the next 18 hours. Fortuitously, dinner tonight is a skewered, barbecued goat.

QE2 continues to be a treat. She sits beside me during the early part of my convalescence and reports on the monkeys that are leaping from branch to branch in the umbrella thorn tree overhead.

"How do they climb so nimbly over those bloody branches with all those ferocious-looking spikes?" she wonders.

Seeing me next to the immaculate QE2, one would never guess that we are on the same trip. My pants are dirty. My fingernails could support plant life. A shower is in order. Plus, I just vomited. She is polo-match perfection in a crisp denim skirt, a pink short-sleeved shirt and spotless white sneakers. She is coiffed, tastefully accessorized and smudge-free. She could knight somebody right here if she found a worthy candidate.

"They must slice themselves up something bloody awful," she decides. "Oh dear, I must attend to my chores."

QE2 is on the Bedford Cleaning Committee, and her royal status offers no exemptions. She leaves me to the monkeys and my sleeping pad. Before passing out on the lawn, I see her inside the truck, a blue scarf wrapped smartly around her head. She wields a broom and sweeps a small cloud of dust out the back of the Bedford with imperial gusto.

In a surprise move, Susan, The Swiss Confectioner and Imodium Overdoser, who was not expected to visit the hole ever again, does just that. But she does not go *in* the hole. She goes in front of me, ergo my surprise.

I am returning to the tent after a series of emergency visits to the officially sanctioned latrine. One extended stop involves an immediate U-turn; I never even make it to the Coca-Cola tree before unbuckling my pants and hobbling back to the hole. Midway through the last visit, a large male baboon appears on a nearby tree branch and studies my every move, redundantly scaring the crap out of me.

Zipping up, I head around the corner and nearly trip over Susan, who is crouching next to a row of bushes. What could she be doing there? Is she hiding from someone?

"Hey," I say.

Then I notice her pants bunched around her ankles and the telltale sound of a deflating whoopee cushion. My interminable monopoly on the hole gave the poor girl no alternative. Eye contact is made, and we share an awkward moment of recognition. She covers her head and apologizes. I shield my eyes and apologize. She tries to make herself invisible, and I try to disappear. I should send a card or something. Does Hallmark have a line for this occasion?

Scott Balows

Returning to the tent, I hear a steady buzz emanating from this end of the damp meadow. The Daft One's soiled tent has become a mecca for a thick cloud of noisy flies.

DAY 9

The Bush Camp to Keratu

After a long night spent seeking the elusive comfortable position, I awake, achy and dehydrated. My body feels glued to the sleeping bag, and I slowly pull myself up on one elbow. This move expends so much effort that I have to lie down and rest for a while. I dress in slow motion, prone on the sleeping pad, elbowing my way into a T-shirt and working my legs into a pair of shorts. One foot is pushed into a Teva, then the other. Closing the Velcro straps is a complex task; rolling over on my stomach and up on my knees is downright Herculean. I slap on deodorant and a hat, and swirl mint toothpaste around a webbed mouth. I am just too tired to wield a toothbrush.

Keeping pace with a dirge, I trudge to the breakfast table, giraffe legs dragging elephant ankles. Gravity is dialed up, and my body tows a Bedford. Every movement is an effort; each gesture is deliberate and glacially paced. Species go extinct while I plod to the campfire. To the surprise of many, I reach the breakfast table under my own power.

"Scott is alive," announces Brian.

"You look like hell," says Judith. "Are you feeling OK?"

"Ugh."

Being sick publicly and belatedly ensures that my piece of the sympathy pie is much larger than if I had gotten sick at the same time as the rest of the group. The slices are accepted with as much grace as possible, but they are not sweet. The worst is behind me, but a long day lies ahead on the same bumpy road we drove in on. On the bright side, I am a member of the club and share an unspoken solidarity with my fellow hurlers.

The breakfast offerings are evaluated for the item with the best odds of outlasting the bumpy ride, but a peanut butter and jelly sandwich hardly passes muster this morning. A few of the British gourmands are slathering baked beans on buttered toast, and Trevor offers me a plate.

"Mmm," I say. "Maybe without the beans. Or the butter."

"You're missing the best parts, mate," says Trevor.

For optimal results, I chew the toast until it is a bland paste. The decision could go either way, but ultimately the small bite of sliced bread stays down.

In all my travels, nothing this bad has ever happened before. My trips have been mostly injury and ailment-free—except for that time in Costa Rica, when I got food poisoning. I was at a lodge in a rain forest near Tortuguero with my sister. A single bite of fried fish activated the saliva floodgates, and a few hours later I was kneeling in front of the hotel room toilet. In the Grand Canyon, a large, wobbly rock rolled over on my shin bone and left a permanent, shallow dent on my left leg. In the Amazon, during a wet six-hour hike through the rain forest, my socks weren't long enough, and the rims of my boots rubbed against my calves so relentlessly, they left identical, bloody divots. While camping alongside the Futaleufu River in Chile, a meadow full of mosquitoes used my big forehead for a salt lick, and the next morning the group thought I had chicken pox. On another river trip, my knees were scraped up one evening when the guides accidentally set the canyon on fire, and I helped extinguish it.

The firefighting adventure begins as T.S. and Mitch, my Zambezi River buddies, and Mitch's fiancée, Sharon, paddle with me through a canyon in southwest Utah. Our four-raft convoy turns off the main river and heads up a chiseled, sky-high gorge, and we pitch our tents on a sliver of isolated beach shadowed by the craggy walls. The camp grows dark after sunset, and three of the guides paddle to the opposite side of the narrow canyon, about 50 yards away. Tonight is the last evening of the final trip of the season, and they are setting up a pyrotechnic display for our viewing pleasure. The dozen guests take seats on the beach and wait while the remaining guide assures us that the spectacle is moments away.

One of the guides ignites a small tin can packed with the trip's used cooking grease, and a sudden flash lights the sky. The can is attached to a string, and he spins it around, shooting a blast of sparks into the night. A fiery trail throws trembling shadows off the stone curtains, and an electric lasso blazes on the water. On the beach, the initial consensus is that we are entertained. Sparks are shooting everywhere; flash pots are going off. It's a little KISS concert right here. Then, a few errant, windblown sparks find kindling along the canyon wall, and the dry scrub brush catches fire, igniting three trees at once. The group is impressed; this is really getting good. Presently, the remaining guide jumps to his feet and starts yelling at us, and we realize this is not part of the show, the part where the canyon goes up in flames.

"Grab buckets! Grab buckets and let's go!" he yells, hurrying to untie one of the rafts.

I toss my camera into my tent and run to the raft. People are darting around; it's Camp Bedlam. The guide is already pushing off when I race into the water and jump inside the raft. Sharon crashes into the front compartment alongside me, and we share "What are we doing here?" expressions. Everyone else is either too late for the guide's urgent timetable or prefers the safety 50 yards of water provides during canyon fires. A couple of well-intentioned guests run up as the guide paddles away, but they can only clutch their kitchen buckets sadly and watch as the brave trio paddles toward the fire, an orange glow shimmering in our wake.

To heighten the absurdity of battling a fire in a national park while on vacation, tonight is Dress-up Night on the river. Dress-up Night is an amusing diversion occasionally encountered on multiday North American rafting trips, wherein the guests assemble costumes from whatever is in their luggage or items they can scavenge. One industrious guest manages a *Playboy* Bunny outfit complete with a unitard, a loofah sponge bunny tail and bunny ears borrowed from a guide. Another guest clear-cuts the shore of undergrowth and fashions a headdress of tall native grasses. T.S. pops out of his tent as though sprung from a jack-in-the-box and lands in front of the group. He is dressed head to toe in black long johns and black river booties, with white paddling gloves, a white bow tie and white suntan lotion coating his face. He is a mime and launches into an inventive and crowd-pleasing routine. He does the bit where he is trapped inside a box, and then an imaginary rope drags him across the beach, none too soon.

Earlier in the day, Mitch and I stumble upon sumo wrestler costumes. We put our life jackets on upside down, with our legs through the armholes, and float into the water, enjoying cold adult beverages beneath the sheer cliff walls. Back onshore, after someone says we resemble ancient Japanese wrestlers, a sumo routine is improvised, complete with grunting, faked Asian expletives and sturdy chest smashing. My life jacket is worn upside down until my thighs start to chafe, then I add a long bandanna tie. This is the extent of my participation in Dress-up Night.

When Sharon leaps into the raft to go firefighting, she is dressed as Carmen Miranda, with bikini bottoms, a towel knotted around her head and another one wrapped strategically across her torso. Mitch dresses as Carmen Miranda's less fetching sister but with a delightfully squeezable padded bosom. When he and T.S. race to the raft with their buckets, they resemble a busty mop woman and Marcel

Marceau standing on the shore. Our guide, meanwhile, dons a bikini top.

He paddles to the other side of the canyon, where the remaining guides, who are dressed as nerds, try to extinguish the fire. The raft dead-ends against the shoreline, a 5-foot rocky wall, and I prepare to de-raft. I decide that it will be more effective to fill the bucket with water first and then leap—Baryshnikov-style—from the raft to the sloping canyon ledge. I dip a large bucket into the river and fill it to the brim, then balance on the raft's inflatable tube and jump to shore. The weight of the bucket functions as an anchor on an ostrich, and that variant goes unfactored in my overall leaping strategy. I crash into the rock wall as expectedly as Wile E. Coyote and claw my way against gravity. Sliding down the ragged cliff, I pull giant rocks on top of my head and plunge into the river. Sputtering, my head breaks the surface of the water, and I gasp for air. I rescue the bucket and pull myself inside the raft.

On the second attempt, I place the full bucket on the ledge first and then jump across. The ground here is steep and rocky, full of narrow ledges and sharp edges, and I am barefoot. I tiptoe gingerly around the jagged and brittle shards with my long bandanna tie trailing behind me. I become useless almost immediately, tripping and sloshing the bucket everywhere but near a flame.

Meanwhile, from the raft, Sharon's full buckets are offered up to the guides as proudly as a hostess with exciting new appetizers. Sharon's breasts are also offered up to the guides when her top towel flaps open in the confusion and excitement, briefly distracting the firenerds from the inferno behind them. I miss this because I am tiptoeing around, falling down, and sloshing water everywhere but near a flame. Sharon's firefighting burlesque act is abruptly terminated and we are ushered back to the raft and returned to camp, since rafting companies frown upon having clients hurt themselves during illegal pyrotechnic displays that go awry in national parks. Fortunately, the fire is soon under control and extinguished. On our arrival back at camp, Mitch poses to Sharon the now immortal question:

"Planning on doing a lot of firefighting in that outfit, honey?"

Meanwhile, back in Africa, the pots and pans need flapping. Not even superhuman displays of hurling excuse me from my kitchen duties, and I join the group to wave plates and bowls in the warm morning air. The dishes are extra heavy today, and the flapping soon approximates a real workout: Sweat pours down my forehead after a few plates, and my arms are tired after a handful of spoons. To minimize the task, some campers hold glasses and kitchenware over the campfire so the heat will evaporate excess moisture. This takes longer than flapping, we discover, after baking our arms over the hot coals. (Lazy flappers are later reprimanded for meals with permanent charred-branch seasoning.)

I don't have much enthusiasm for dish drying today and return to the tent for a nap before packing my campsite. My grim state promises to make the task a lengthy one, and I wonder where that

Maasai Tent Warrior is when I need him. The first stage involves spreading the sleeping bag on the tent floor, grabbing it by the heel and shoving it inside a gear sack. The sleeping bag is made of resilient material, however, and does not wish to be tied up inside a small, dark sack. It rebounds after every handful, determined to force its way out. Such negligible progress is being made that I lie on my back, hold the sack with both hands and pedal the sleeping bag inside with my legs. Inch by reluctant inch, the seven-foot-long bag disappears. I cinch off the gear sack and rest.

Next, I unscrew the nozzle of my sleeping pad and flatten my body atop it, humping out excess air until it is mostly deflated. One end is folded over a few inches and more air is pressed out. This process is repeated another 20 times until the inflatable mattress is rolled into a tight, nearly airless tube. I kneel atop it to prevent the pad from unspooling and reach for another gear sack. I try to force the pad inside but it is too big; not enough air has been removed. I would have better luck coaxing a baby hippo in there.

The entire process has to be repeated. The flattening. The humping. The deflating. The folding. The pressing. The repeating. The rolling. The kneeling. The preventing. The reaching. The forcing. By the time the mattress is rolled into an even tighter tube, I am dripping sweat, and the drizzled pad is slipped inside the gear sack—this time with success. I cinch it off and rest.

Dirty clothes and toiletries are rounded up and tossed inside a kit; lens tissue and rolls of film are zipped inside a camera bag. I crawl out of the tent and circle the perimeter, stopping every few feet to unlatch the loops that attach the tent fly to the stakes. The dew-covered tarp is wrestled off the tent and spread atop the lawn to dry. Six metal stakes secure the tent, and I squat down in front of each one to yank it from the ground. The stakes are firmly encased in a thick muck, however, and will not give without effort. The third one comes free after a two-handed jerk, and the surprising momentum rolls me backward onto the muddy lawn, legs in the air. The remaining stakes are collected with less flailing; I cinch them off inside a small sack and rest.

I grab the tent poles with both hands and—like Atlas hoisting the globe—raise the large but lightweight tent high above my head so it appears, briefly, that I have superhuman powers other than hurling. I shake out trash and dirt and lower the tent to the grass. The Velcro latches that secure the tent to the poles are unhooked and the tent collapses. The poles are pulled out of their loops, taken apart and slipped inside a bag. The tent and the fly are laid flat atop the grass, and the sides are folded into thirds.

The final stage, where the tent, the fly, the poles and the stakes are wrapped into a tight Mexican delicacy, is not completed until after several false starts. An awkward wrestling match follows as the unruly tent burrito is ensnared inside the largest gear sack. The tent gains the upper hand almost immediately by unraveling from the top, and the two of us tip over onto the wet ground. Kneeling atop the unwieldy bundle, I clutch it between my thighs and slowly inch the gear sack over the tent. From a distance, it appears that I am fornicating outdoor gear. The tent finally slips inside. I cinch it off and collapse.

A slow parade of sick guests carry their gear to the Bedford and begin an enervated rendition of the pre-departure ritual. We fumble with keys and dig into cubbyholes, exchanging dirty clothes for less dirty ones. On the lawn, Trevor and a nearby monkey distract the group with a rendition of monkey-see, monkey-do. Or Trevor-see, Trevor-do; it is anyone's guess, really. Trevor hunkers down; the monkey hunkers down. The monkey bounces on his haunches; Trevor bounces on his haunches. Trevor stands up; the monkey stands up. Although the group is nauseous and lethargic, we still know what's funny and laugh in spite of how crappy we feel.

As backpacks and water bottles are stored atop the shelves overhead, someone pulls a bowl of vegetables from a cubbyhole for today's lunch. They smell horrible.

"Whew, I believe those vegetables have seen better days," says Janet.

"Oh, they're bloody awful," agrees Selena.

"Well, I don't fancy we'll be eating them," says Janet. "I can barely keep my food down as it is."

A brief debate begins on the fate of the vegetables, but it is mostly one-sided. The Daft One is aboard the Bedford at the time of the discussion, and when he leaves the bad-vegetable odor follows him off the truck.

"That's odd. The vegetables don't smell anymore," says Janet.

Selena sniffs the air and agrees. "I think it might have been Steve."

The group has no choice but to let the lettuce, peppers and carrots off with just a warning and declare The Daft One guilty of smelling. Tim, who deserves an award for informing someone that they smell in the kindest way possible, follows The Daft One off the truck and politely informs him that he is malodorous.

"Steve, you have a bit of an aroma about you today," says Tim. "Not hard to do out here, what with no showers and all."

Tim is generous and nonaccusatory, and you almost wish you had a nasty funk oozing from your pores if you knew the matter would be handled with such delicacy. Before the Bedford pulls out of the bush camp, The Daft One claims a seat in the back of the truck and apologizes for smelling. The odor is similar to the one that greeted me inside the hotel room the first night: a pungent funk of sweat and old milk, only worse. He smells like a man who used his sleeping bag for a loo and forgot to flush.

The Bedford drives through a dusty ghost town of roofless brick houses and parks outside a small store with ornamental windowpanes. A tall kid in a long blue sweater swings from a rusty white pole, and half a dozen young boys join him beneath the store's ruffled tin eaves. The kids monitor the truck for signs of potential Godlike behavior, such as a tourist fishing around a backpack for a spare pen. Several people climb down from the truck to stock up on bottled water and snacks, and the delay increases the tension for the anxious youngsters.

"Are the kognyogi brothers coming down for a fresh supply?" asks Janet.

"I would imagine. They've been drinking it like water," says Selena.

"They certainly do fancy it, don't they?"

Kognyogi is the African equivalent of gin and is the main ingredient in Trevor and Brian's favorite safari cocktail. They've been buying enough quantities of it here for the past two days to earn them the aforementioned moniker. The storekeeper will be sad to see them leave, no doubt posting his finest quarterly sales ever.

"It probably explains why they're still healthy," I say. "Their stomachs are so toxic, the germs don't stand a chance."

"Tim, be a dear and grab me a bottle of that kognyogi," says Janet.

Sometimes kognyogi is only available in plastic packets, resembling to-go ketchup or take-out sweet-and-sour sauce, and Brian and Trevor rip the containers open with their teeth and mix them with 7-Up. The stuff is an acquired taste, if you ask me, and my loyalty stays true to whatever beer is the least lukewarm. While we wait for the kognyogi brothers to climb aboard, the kids turn their devotion toward Valerie as she parts with a handful of pens.

"Here you go," she yells, leaning out the truck and tossing half a dozen ballpoints from the elevated window.

The pens fly skyward and hang in midair, spinning and twirling in the morning sun. The boys jostle for position beneath them and elbow their neighbors out of the way with sharp jabs. The pens rain down from the sky, slipping through clumsy hands and bouncing off outstretched arms. Pen giving is never quite as dignified as when QE2 bequeaths them. There is no grace or order here, and the seamy underside of unrestricted pen tossing is exposed.

They spill to the ground, and a game of smear-the-queer-with-the-pen breaks out. The kids grab at loose shirts and punch their friends for a foreign Bic. They slam their little brothers to the ground and tear pens out of each other's hands. One lucky boy emerges with a writing utensil and holds it aloft; he is tackled to the dirt and swarmed instantly. The kids are as vicious as hungry hyenas fighting over a gazelle, snapping and snarling at one another to claim a pen.

Marc videotapes the scene and narrates in French: *"Valerie a lancé seulement un paquet de stylos aux petits enfants et maintenant ils battent le crap de l'un a l'autre."* In French, of course, it does not sound as though the young boys are beating the crap out of each other, but as though they are sipping wine or painting flowers.

There are not enough pens to go around, so when the dust settles, elation and crushing disappointment mix as the victors skip off with their prizes, and the empty-handed search our faces for just one more pen.

My pants aren't just dirty.

"They're gross," says Judith.

That is the Brit's near-unanimous decision regarding my mottled trousers, and they are openly mocked.

"How did you get them so filthy?" asks Tony.

"What have you been doing, Scott?" asks Janet.

"Are you rolling around in the mud?" asks Roy.

"Did you go for a swim in the hole?" asks Selena.

The Brits cannot believe how gross my pants are, and frankly, they are a little disgusted. But not surprised, seeing as how it's The Yank and all. The fact that we are on a camping trip in Africa and pants are going to get a little dirty in the daily course of wrestling tents, dodging dust storms and hurling in the bush is not considered in their brusque evaluation.

A little perspective here: These same people have seen a lion stick his head inside the body cavity of a dead Cape buffalo, emerge with internal organs in his blood-caked mouth, and they have been captivated. They have seen baboons pick the fleas out of each other's inflamed baboon butts and eat them, and deemed it cute. They have crapped with a dozen diarrheic strangers in a communal hole, mind you, without complaint.

But my pants? *They're gross.*

With a flash of Yankee ingenuity, I zip the legs off and make the most offensive parts of my pants disappear.

The Bedford heads north toward Keratu, about halfway between Lake Manyara and Ngorongoro Crater. Our destination is nicknamed Safari Junction and is a common stop for outfitters stocking up on supplies before heading into the Serengeti. We drive through the sunbaked town, past stores with bright turquoise shutters and a post office fronted by zebra-print stone columns. The townspeople push bikes through the streets and gather on wooden benches next to Styrofoam coolers. Accompanied by the stoic gazes of many locals, the truck follows a dead-end dirt road to a campground surrounded by a sparse community of unfinished brick buildings and ringed by a fence of thick hedges. Straw-tossed campsites lined with trees flank a small house, and gravel paths allow for jeeps and giant trucks to navigate the compound.

Elevated flush toilets and working showers are the most popular features of a brick cottage, which also has a dining room, a small bar, a reception nook and living quarters for the owners. Landscaped gardens full of purple flowers and cushioned Adirondack chairs surround the house. Centering the campsite is The Daft One's soiled tent, and the fragrant memento hangs from a sagging clothesline that ripples in the warm breeze. An unlucky camp employee approaches it reluctantly, under-armed with a bucket of sudsy water and a mop, and begins to scrub.

Meanwhile, I attempt to launder my pants into some shade of respectability; they're pretty gross. The laundromat is a cement block with an upside down J-faucet and a drain in the center. The washbasin sits across from the hedge fence and a brick gazebo with grills and countertops. A smaller brick shed with hole-in-the-floor bathrooms sits on the opposite side. Behind this is a neighbor's home with a yard full of chickens, which occasionally poke their heads between the hedges to see what I'm up to. Beyond the fence is an unpaved road bordered by acres of sloping farmland and tilled dirt rows.

I fill a large plastic bowl with water and biodegradable camp suds, and submerge the grimy pants. The water turns black almost instantly, and four cycles later, the mixture still resembles a cow blood latte. Cleanliness being next to godliness, it is here—while washing zip-off Eddie Bauer hiking pants in the middle of Tanzania and an atheist-proof sunset, the sky a smear of plum and orange—that the Lord speaks to me.

"Alo?" says the Lord, "Alo?"

The voice comes from the shrub fence in front of me, but no one is there. Just as God appeared to Moses as a burning bush, the Lord speaks to me through the flora. My illness has subsided, so this is either Larium-induced psychosis or the fifth delusion. God is a hedge. A giant green hedge.

"*Jambo,*" I reply, glancing around to see if anyone notices me talking to the bushes. "How ya doin'?"

What could the Lord want of me, a simple traveler here in Africa?

"Do you have a pen?" He says.

God wants a pen. An extra commandment, perhaps. God also has the voice of a 5-year-old boy, who is now visible crouching on the ground behind the bushy fence and sticking his head between the hedges like a shy chicken.

"Alo. Do you have a pen?" he asks again.

"A pen?" I say. "No. No pens."

I don't have the heart to tell the kid that I have a handful of the coolest pens ever at the other end of the campsite. They're right over there, aboard that big truck, locked inside a cubbyhole and sealed away inside an envelope at the bottom of a duffel bag. But I'm doing laundry right now; not a good time to be doling out the Bics. With audible remorse, it occurs to me that I will never be a pen-giving deity if I won't give one to the kid who for a second I thought was God.

After draping a tree with damp laundry, I head across the campsite to the main house and the small bar. Trevor and Brian have already staked out strategic positions near a red cooler filled to the brim with a colorful mix of frosty beers. The admiration of the cooler is a testament to the body's recuperative powers and—in spite of feeling like a pen-hoarding jerk—I feel almost human. The bug must have been the less-than-24-hour variety, and my thorough purging expelled most of the nasty bits. I am well enough to nurse a Castle Lager with Trevor and Brian—who is celebrating his 50th birthday today—and Tony, Selena and Judith over several fierce games of cards in the garden. It is a quality afternoon, for some. Many guests are showing no signs of improvement, and more are dropping faster than injured antelopes. The latest victim is QE2, who stays inside her tent with a cold compress all afternoon. The Brits, as you might imagine, are concerned that their monarch is not feeling well.

"She might need to go to the hospital," says Selena.

By the time the story speeds through camp, QE2 is near death, and a priest is on his way. Roy is not pleased about this turn of events; he is even less excited about the next news flash, which offers a valid explanation for our epidemic ailment. After cleaning up for dinner, I find most of the group gathered around the Bedford. The mood is tense and agitated. Tony approaches me and says, "Steve did it."

"What?"

"He filled the water jug."

"The one with the colored shoelace," says Janet.

"He didn't tell the guides," says Tony. "It wasn't treated."

"He's been handling our water?"

"Juma saw him. I remember it too. At the Lake Manyara campsite, the night before everyone got sick."

"That bastard made us all sick," adds Roy. "I'm going to kill him."

This water jug is the one we drink from, the one we use for dishwashing and preparing food. No doubt, people drank from the jug or ate food cooked and cleaned in it. By all accounts, The Daft One has inadvertently poisoned us, and we still have another week together. The rumble of dissension spreads through camp; people are *knarcky*. The group resembles the angry, pitchfork-wielding townsfolk who live down the hill from Dr. Frankenstein's castle, only we have Swiss army knives. A small mob gathers around the Bedford as Kinyua averts a minor group uprising by belatedly relieving The Daft One of his water-bearing duties. He responds with a disinterested, incoherent bluster and climbs aboard the truck. Roy really might kill him; he will not have to look far for accomplices.

That evening, I grab a pen from the bottom of my duffel bag and go looking for God.

Shortly after determining that The Daft One is responsible for infecting us with a water-transported parasite, we sit down to dinner together in the campground's restaurant for a family-style meal. The restaurant resembles a large dining room in a warm home, with hardwood floors, framed photos and a trio of small round tables pushed together. The Daft One sits in the middle (next to QE2, who is healthy enough to eat dinner and does not require last rites), while the rest of the group fans around as far away as possible.

Today may be Brian's 50th birthday, but this surprise feast is on his shilling, and for the first time in a week, we don't eat with plates on our laps. We use napkins and prop our elbows on the blue-and-white checked tablecloths. Baskets of dinner rolls are passed around, and water glasses seem to fill by themselves. The buffet of roasted chicken, baked potatoes, steamed veggies and warm bread sprawls out against one wall and is our most memorable and awkward meal. During the entire dinner, The Daft One neither speaks nor is spoken to; he is only spoken about.

"Did you hear him say we only needed one photo of the baby elephant?" asks Tony.

"The guy sat by himself at the welcome dinner. That's all you need to know," I say.

"Well, remember which sleeping pad is yours. His has shit all over it," Roy advises.

"He's not such a bad guy," says Tim.

The Daft One leaves after dessert. Our dishes begin to disappear and some people experience flapping withdrawals, instinctively grabbing for forgotten bread plates. Most of the group stays up late, playing cards and contributing to Brian's 50th birthday hangover. We take over the house and keep the staff confused with multiple bar tabs. Somehow, the night deteriorates, and Brian cuffs me upside the head and plants a sloppy kiss on my cheek, in quick succession. A British expression of endearment, I'm guessing.

Long after the bar closes, closer to dawn, the wind dies and the campground grows quiet. All through the tents, not a sleeping bag is stirring. Nary a breeze disturbs the damp T-shirts and towels that hang from the tree branches. No birds interrupt the eerie silence. A few moments before the sun, someone begins to scream, quietly at first. The moan comes to life and reaches across the farmlands that surround the campsite. The cry increases in volume and torment, and it sounds as though Roy is killing The Daft One, by strangulation, perhaps. This is a voice in pain. Then a crowd joins in and the sound of a hundred tortured voices wails inside my tent. The screams echo in the background of a Larium-enhanced dream and roust me from a solid sleep.

"Oooom," they wail, a flock of kori bustards with bullhorns.

The voices are not coming from my head this time but from across the tilled rows. There is a mosque beyond the hedges, and a congregation gathers for an early-morning mass. The members are praying—probably not a bad idea.

DAY 10

Keratu to the Serengeti National Park

The middle of the Serengeti is a five-hour drive away, and Tim and I continue to study our Swahili numbers.

"*Mo-jaw. Mbee-lee. Ta-too. Naw-nee,*" Tim says.

"*Mo-jaw. Mbee-lee. Ta-too. Naw-nee,*" I repeat.

The Bedford climbs the Rift Valley Ridge and heads southwest toward Ngorongoro Crater. Vast and sparsely populated, the plains and steppes of this part of Tanzania are just that: a tectonic staircase that rises from the coast and over the Eastern Rift Valley to the Ngorongoro highlands.

"Five is *taw-noh.*"

"*Taw-noh.*"

"Six is *see-taw.*"

"*See-taw.*"

The crater is the world's largest unbroken caldera and was formed more than 2 million years ago when a volcano blew up and collapsed on itself. The blast left a 2,000-foot-deep, stone-lined basin that stretches 12 miles across at its widest.

"Seven is *saw-baw.*"

"*Saw-baw. Taw-noh, see-taw, saw-baw.*"

"*Mo-jaw. Mbee-lee. Ta-too. Naw-nee. Taw-noh. See-taw. Saw-baw.*"

A plateau forms the rim, and the high elevation creates weather conditions that are so cold and foggy, we can see our breath but little else. Tony, Selena, Judith and I continue to play ruthless games of spades and hearts, while the rest of the group digs through their cubbyholes for warmer clothes, reads about Maasai customs or stares ahead blankly. Driving around a curve, the Bedford swerves into sunlight and the climate shifts from San Francisco's to L.A.'s; the weather is sunny and warm. As our layers of fleece are stripped off, a sliver of crater flashes us through a bare spot in the dense woods.

Ngorongoro is right there.

A swath is cut in the thick ring of foliage that borders the crater rim, and the Bedford arrives at a scenic overlook carved out of a steep hill. We climb off the truck for our first complete views and race to the edge, where a sloping briar patch of tangled shrubs and windswept trees disappears beneath our feet. An immense chunk of earth has been scooped out of the ground and painted in shades of green and gold, and a giant lake centers the crater like a blue iris in a misshapen eye. The entire basin is visible from rim to rim, and it is massive and compact at the same time. The place looks deserted; you'd never guess that there are 25,000 animals down there.

Across much of the opposite side, a thick layer of fog rolls across the terrain. It obscures the trees and cascades over the rim, pouring into the crater in slow motion. The spectacle resembles Victoria Falls in cloud form, and I am suitably impressed.

"That is one big hole."

Then, a trio of Maasai men approaches, and their remarkable earlobes overshadow the Eighth Wonder of the World. The Ngorongoro highlands are the warriors' centuries-old pastoral home, and they have a settlement over the next rise. The men also have earlobes of unimaginable shape and size. One epic pair dangles on blanket-covered shoulders like pencil-thick strands of looping Silly Putty, stretched so far and wide you could drive a toy truck through them. Another man has shredded and twisted his lobes into the fringe from a Persian rug. The third man has a large aspirin bottle—60-caplet-size—wedged inside a hole in his earlobe, medicine cabinet space being what it is these days. I grab for a lobe and experience another bout of Instantaneous Phantom Ear Pain.

"Do you get phantom ear pain out here?" I ask Tim as the red-blanketed Maasai men disappear behind a ridge.

"Phantom ear pain? I don't believe I'm familiar with that."

"When you see a guy with a big hole in his ear, it makes you grab your own ear?"

"No, I don't. Did you just have a spell?"

"Yeah."

"Well, this would be the place for it."

As the Bedford descends from the crater rim, Selena reads to us about Maasai circumcision ceremonies, and suddenly Instantaneous Phantom Ear Pain does not sound so bad.

"The second and most important initiation, is *Emuratare*, the circumcision," she reads.

"Selena—" says Tony.

"Such an operation is not pleasant," she continues. "It is very painful."

"I bet. They're 10 years old," I say.

"Yet it means a lot to every Maasai. A boy will prove that he is ready to be initiated by exhibiting signs of a grown man, such as carrying a heavy spear—"

"Bollocks, I dropped the spear," says Tony.

"—and taking care of the livestock."

"Dang, I lost the cows," I say.

"The operation takes place in the early dawn shortly before sunrise," continues Selena.

"Right, before they've had coffee," says Tony.

"It is performed by a qualified man who administers no medications or numbing agents."

"Thomas, how do you say 'anesthesia' in Swahili?" I ask.

"After the operation is completed, the boy receives gifts of livestock."

"Great. They chop off his foreskin and he gets a cow."

"Tony would only get a calf," adds Selena.

The Ngorongoro highlands taper off as the Rift Valley ridge swoops down to the Serengeti plains. Kinyua barely turns the wheel over the course of the next 250 miles and drives straight across an endless grassy field that resembles the Midwest, save for a handful of hyenas and the occasional ostrich. Thomas continues to be quick on the buzzer.

"How big is the Serengeti?"

"Almost 15,000 square kilometers."

(That's about 9,000 miles. Almost as big as Vermont.)

"When is the wildebeest migration?"

"Between December and July."

"How do you tell the Thomson's gazelle from the Grant's gazelle?"

"Grants are bigger and paler."

"Where is everybody?"

There is hardly anybody to wave to here, except for the tall grass that waves back hypnotically and lulls the group into a savanna stupor. I look out at the Serengeti's grasslands and conjure lions, cheetahs, leopards, hyenas, elephants, hippopotami, wildebeests, zebras, buffaloes, waterbucks, warthogs, rhinos, baboons, dikdiks, antelopes, gazelles, giraffes, wild dogs, bat-eared foxes, crocodiles, over 500 species of birds and 100 species of busy dung beetles.

Another chapter of *Hannibal* is finished, and by now the man-eating forest hogs are being packed inside specially designed crates and shipped to America. They are going to eat the mad doctor, beginning with his feet. The pigs will dine on him slowly, and he will be kept alive to witness his bloody demise. Tony and I are both reading the same book and warn each other about the atrocities to come.

We play more cards, watch the unchanging scenery pass by and contemplate our neighbors. The Daft One sits across from me and stares ahead from vacant eyes, disengaged and expressionless. He looks to be about as happy as a dung beetle, or the aardwolf, a diminutive relative of the hyena, whose teeth are too small for killing or chewing, and must subsist on a specialized diet of termites.

Enduring long stretches in close quarters with him is a plot twist almost too absurd to be believed. The guy makes us all sick and now we're going to drive across Africa with him? But he has isolated himself from the group since the welcome dinner, and—other than infecting us with a water-based parasite—he has mostly succeeded. He rarely makes conversation or interacts; he never hikes. His minimal social requirements have been accommodated from the outset, so by now our indifference is second nature. For the most part, the group handles the situation with the composure of responsible adults. The urban Brits, as depicted in many of their small, independent films, are witty and well-mannered. No one has tried to behead the bloke, and we haven't had a group uprising since last night. I even include him in a game of cards, but he declines.

Then we spot our first cheetah and forget all about the guy.

Thomas spies her with some sort of freakish cheetah-ray vision. Standing at the back of the Bedford, he gazes out the window and scans the horizon with well-trained eyes. He finds the cat beneath a shaded tree, behind tall grass the same color as she is, at least 60 yards from the road. Taking advantage of the Bedford's all-wheel drive, Kinyua heads off road and drives within a respectable distance of the cheetah, the golden-haired supermodel of the Serengeti. The cat has long legs and a sleek, toned figure peppered with dark beauty marks. She sprawls beneath the tree, haughty and indifferent, and ignores us. She twitches an ear. Looks right, left. Breathes.

This is enough, a cheetah lying under a tree.

Kinyua joins us in the back of the truck and delivers The Serengeti Safety Orientation. He explains that our next campsite, unlike earlier ones that spoiled us with gift shops, spear-wielding Maasai Warriors and fences, has no fences. The campground is just that: a parcel of grassland to set our tents on. There is nobody to discourage the carnivores from strolling into camp and tearing through our tents. Nothing to dissuade them from ripping us out of our sleeping bags and eating us alive. In a food chain competition, we would not crack the top five.

"OK? All right," says Kinyua.

This is not all right to Minouk.

"There are no fences?" she asks, glancing around to see if anyone else thinks this is a security oversight. "Is that safe?"

"Don't worry," Kinyua assures her. "People are hardly ever eaten."

He explains that hyenas will enter the camp on occasion and scope out the tastiest campers from beneath the truck.

"But they probably won't bother you," Kinyua says. "OK? All right."

"What if we have to go to the bathroom?" Minouk asks.

"Go in a group," Kinyua says.

"With a slower and more delicious guest," I add. "Preferably someone smeared with antelope."

"And take your torch," Kinyua advises.

While "torch" might sound vaguely ominous and imply a flame-based deterrent of some caliber, it is just the British word for *flashlight*. Like you would have at home in a drawer. There is no flammability involved of any kind.

"But don't worry," Kinyua says. "Just point your torch in the animal's face and jostle it in his eyes. It will run away. OK? All right."

This is news to me, and I watch a lot of *Animal Planet*. But apparently, Africa's most ferocious predators have an irrational fear of wobbly light beams. To alleviate any concerns, Kinyua will sleep on the cushioned seat in the Bedford's balcony, 20 feet off the ground.

The truck arrives at the Seronera Lodge, an architectural jumble constructed around a *koppie* (pronounced koh-pee), one of the occasional rocky islands that jut out from the plains. The hotel has the ramshackle quality of a tree house whose shape is dictated by the house-size obelisks poking through the roof. The stairways and common areas are wrapped around giant boulders, and we spend the afternoon exploring the cavernous hallways and relaxing on an elevated stone patio with humbling views of a vast grassy ocean. The Maasai described the place perfectly when they named it: Serengeti means "the land that does not end."

Tim and Janet, as well as Marc and Valerie, decide to part with a few shillings in exchange for a real bed, a hot shower and a toilet that does not involve digging one. Tomorrow is a full day in the Serengeti after all, and everyone wants to feel their best.

By the time the group departs the hotel for our fenceless campground, the sun is setting and lions and hyenas are howling in the distance. Campsites are staked out quickly and positioned close to the fire. Nobody wants his or her tent to be the first line of defense, so we sacrifice privacy for safety and cluster together. We race around faster than Maasai Tent Warriors and set them up in record time, as though the nylon dwellings are claw-resistant, and we will be safe inside.

Tonight is my turn for kitchen duty and I chop vegetables for a Bolognese sauce. The night is unmatched: The repartee is quick-witted and good-spirited; the beers are lukewarm—a Lion Lager is killed as a sacrifice to the park's number one predator—the stars outnumber the wildebeests and I am dicing tomatoes in the Serengeti. Soon, the smell of an Italian feast—of garlic bread and a tangy sauce—mingles with the scent of nervous prey and exotic manure. They blend into an intoxicating aroma that is earthy and pungent, basil and buffalo.

Keeping the group company is a large bat that flies reconnaissance missions above our heads, searching for his dinner. The bat alights on a slim branch above the tomato-chopping table, and our flashlights find him as he shoves a bug in his mouth. He stops in mid chew and releases the branch with his leathery talons. Without warning, the kamikaze bat makes a beeline for my head and uses my nose for a bull's-eye. My logical response is to duck and cover.

"Look at him go," says Judith.

"That's the fastest The Yank's moved the entire trip," adds Trevor.

The group insists that the bat did not come anywhere near me and that diving under a table is a typically extreme, American response. I remain steadfast that this is not Delusion no. 6—I was just strafed by a flying rat. Man-eating lions and crocodile-infested rivers I'm OK with. Bats? Nobody mentioned bats.

The collection of fated adventurers bonds around our mutual hurling and wildlife encounters. Our chairs are arranged around the campfire in a close circle, and the familiarity of our good-natured ribbing belies the fact that we have known each other a week. As these kinds of trips typically progress, whenever strangers drive around and look at wild animals together, the fire grows warmer; our circle grows tighter.

For everyone, that is, but The Daft One.

He places his chair next to the truck, away from the circle, and leans against the Bedford. A truck sconce throws a dramatic spotlight over his head, and the campfire reflects off his thick glasses, turning his eyes into twin flames. Thomas keeps him company, and his occasional laughter suggests that The Daft One is a formidable wit or that Thomas is a great guy.

The Daft One makes an efficient scapegoat. He doesn't sit with us at the welcome dinner. He complains about the camp rules and then ignores them. He never seems to know or care when it is his turn to do the dishes or help in the kitchen. He smells. He even blames the wildlife for not being photogenic enough. The elephants are looking the wrong way or the lion won't open his eyes. In fact, there does not appear to be a single aspect of the safari he finds agreeable. But, the rules of travel dictate that one annoying person must attend every trip, and The Daft One is ours.

A man on the recent Zambezi trip was a protégé of The Daft One. During a break on the river, he asked my friend T.S. for a sip of water from his jug. He took a long drink, poured the rest of it on his feet and handed the water bottle back empty. This same man initiated the traffic jam that caused our guide on the Zambezi to utter the now immortal phrase, "This is not a good time to fuck up." There was this woman in the Galapagos Islands who refused to learn how to flush the toilet on our small boat and would repeatedly call for her husband to flush it for her. "Honey, I'm done," she would announce during lunch, and he would stop eating and rush downstairs to flush the toilet. On a sea kayaking trip in Baja, when one of the tourists was over-served at

137

a margarita happy hour, he stumbled into an open manhole and bled all over another guest's hotel room. Wait, that was me.

At the opposite end of these bozos is a guy such as Tim who continues to demonstrate the tolerance and compassion of Mother Teresa. He pulls up a chair next to The Daft One and tells him that not everybody hates him.

The spotted hyenas are the hollow-eyed, black-faced burn victims of the Serengeti. They have the distinction of not having plush toys made in their likeness. What they do enjoy are some of the most powerful, antelope-shredding jaws in the animal kingdom. Typically characterized as lowly scavengers, hyenas are actually expert predators of animals as large as a zebra; in some regions they even dominate the lions. This suggests that my tent, weighing in at five millimeters of nylon, will not be a worthy adversary.

A hyena is watching me now. The red glow of his eyes reflected in the torch's beam stares back, and the twin embers hover above the grass as he slinks closer. All that separates us is 20 yards of sparsely wooded grassland and the double-stitched reassurance of my tent. Kinyua's torch-jostling instructions appear particularly ineffective: I am jostling to beat the bushes here, but the hyena is unfazed and continues to approach. He appears, in fact, to make a mental note about which tent belongs to the annoying torch jostler. I retreat to the safety of the campfire with its large selection of slower, more delicious guests.

For much of the night, the group patrols the campground where the light trails off, and the strange sounds and flickering shadows play tricks. Every piece of dry brush trampled underfoot has us searching for wildlife. A rustling in the grass leads to visions of carnivores; a snapped branch must be a stalking lion. The night is scoured for glowing eyes, and several animals are revealed. Two hyenas circle the camp, and a small monkey perches in a tree branch. A mongoose-shaped animal with a low body and a long tail slinks into camp and climbs atop a nearby Land Rover to warm itself on the hood. We keep a silent vigil and feed the fire late into the evening to see if any hyenas are bold enough to breach the campsite and watch us from beneath the truck.

"Do you hear that?" says Minouk. "I think I hear something."

The group quiets and turns a collective ear as something crashes through the underbrush.

"Something's out there."

We jump to our feet and race to the edge of the campsite with our torches blazing and shoot beams of light across the savanna like helicopter searchlights.

"What is it?"

"It's over there."

"No, over there."

There it is. A tall, upright figure emerges from the darkness. Is it a clumsy giraffe? A lion walking on its hind legs? The creature comes closer and appears disoriented. It wanders aimlessly. It speaks.

"Is this the bathroom?" she asks.

It is The Daft One's female counterpart: a delirious middle-aged woman walking around the Serengeti alone in the dark.

"Is she daft?" Tony wonders.

"Natural selection at work," I say.

"It is not a good idea to be wandering around the Serengeti alone in the dark," says Selena.

"Is the bathroom over here?" she asks.

She is assured that our campfire is not the bathroom, and directions are provided to the nearest latrine.

Before going to bed, I crawl around the outside of my tent and pull up two metal tent stakes, just in case lions attack during the night. Best to be prepared, I say. I place the stakes next to my sleeping bag and practice finding them in the dark.

DAY 11

The Serengeti National Park

I discover too late that my tent sits above a termite mound in the exploratory stages, and throughout the night, the busy insects remove dirt from their miniature mineshaft and hurl it against the floor. The acoustics amplify the excavation and the sound is of a biblical hailstorm passing through. When that doesn't have me bolting upright in the sleeping bag, the cackling hyenas wake me with a jolt. I grab for tent stakes but find myself armed only with mint dental floss.

At 5:00 A.M., the tent is unzipped and I slip out the doorway. The sky is pitch-black and the campsite is quiet. I point my torch into the bush and search for glowing orbs, but there is no evidence of stalking predators. Then I hear a low grumble behind me. A pair of wobbly beams reveals an approaching jeep—not a bloodthirsty lion—and it comes to a stop in our camp. Tony, Selena and I climb inside and drive off. Five more guests are picked up from a neighboring campsite, and the jeep disappears down a shadowy road. At a nearby juncture, the driver hits the brakes and comes to an abrupt stop, as though he's missed an exit, or worse, lost. Great. Middle of the night. The Serengeti. Lost. The driver shifts into reverse, backs up 10 feet and stops again. The guy has no idea where he's going.

The glow from the headlights illuminates the road in front of us and the tall grass on either side. On cue, the massive adult male lion the driver spotted a moment earlier lifts his head above the swaying prairie and glares at us from a few feet away. This is a movie star—caliber lion, with a classically shaped head and a full crown of golden mane. A steady breeze blows the thick fur away from his face and reveals a magnificent, chiseled profile. He is in his prime, confident and unflinching, and the headlights paint him in a heroic glow. He regards the jeep's passengers like a feline Clint Eastwood, squinting back at us with a sleepy sneer across his face.

"Lion!" someone in the Land Rover says aloud, the guy in the front seat, The Guy Who Will Point Out Clearly Visible Animals. I even gesture at it, should the other passengers be experiencing any difficulty pinpointing a big, glaring, adult male lion that is directly in front of us. I can't help it; I am a human GPS, only for wildlife. In my mind, a valuable public service is being provided— Delusion no. 6.

The jeep travels another half mile and parks. In the semidarkness, the passengers climb out in the middle of an expansive plain, the same sort of grassy plain preferred by big, glaring, adult male lions. The group does not wander off. Two large, embryonic, green-and-khaki-striped forms billow on the ground, and two dozen people mill about in small groups. Abruptly, a thick Southern accent shatters the unique silence of the Serengeti in the moments before dawn.

"Hey y'all, this big ol' termite mound is gonna be the potty spot. I'm gonna have myself a pee, so if y'all don't want to be a-lookin' at my big white fanny, don't be a-lookin' this way," she broadcasts to every creature within miles.

Rest assured, all the termites in Tanzania working diligently as a team could not build a mound large enough to obscure any region of this woman's spacious, cheese 'n' grits—fed fanny. Tony turns to me with typically deft timing and says, "This is why we make fun of Americans on holiday."

The dawn's early light crests the horizon. The skyline ignites and an orange glow creeps over the edges, marking the clouds with purple bruises. The night withdraws, and a long, spindly fence of acacia trees is silhouetted in the distance. The tip of the sun backlights the scene, and it is the world's largest postcard. Then the laws of gravity fail and the earth lets go.

Weightless, I hover above the ground, skimming the treetops and floating into the sky. This is not a Larium dream but a hot air balloon ride over the Serengeti at sunrise. A miniature flamethrower tops our wicker basket and the pilot shoots long tongues of fire above our heads. The flames lick the balloon material, and one cannot help but notice that *the flames are licking the balloon material.* Apparently, this is no cause for alarm, and the balloon ascends without igniting.

A dark cover is peeled away and a slight breeze shoots patterns across the grass, turning the savanna into a sheet of rippled gold. A long green swatch of acacia trees hugs the banks of a narrow stream, and budding, amber-colored foothills surf the horizon's edge. The whole thing is just ridiculously stunning.

A male lion, the same one pointed out before, glares up at us now. A vulture and her nest are viewed from the top, for a change. Fifty or more hippos, resembling tiny bath toys, bob around a crowded watering hole. The migration paths left a few months earlier by two million wildebeests are revealed by long slash marks in the dry earth. A small herd of skittish zebras runs away now, terrified. In spite of seven years of daily flights without a single balloon-related zebra fatality, the zebras awake each morning with their sense of hot air balloon fear renewed, and they flee across the plains.

The balloon is a slow-motion roller-coaster ride, dropping toward the earth and brushing the treetops before soaring a thousand feet in the air. The pilot navigates the open sky and drifts above a narrow road that meanders through the park, playing a game of cat and gazelle behind a companion balloon. A mother and baby giraffe nibble on the rich leaves of an acacia tree; a jackal grooms himself.

In the distance, an engine's rumble and a cloud of dust indicate an approaching jeep, and a large truck filled with tourists follows behind. It's the Bedford! The Bedford is headed straight for us. I want to make certain that the truck's passengers notice the large hot air balloon floating 50 feet above their heads, so I lean out the basket and wave fanatically.

"*Jambo! Jambo!*"

They see us: The truck's excited passengers wave back from the open windows. The balloon sails above the truck and aims for the clouds; my lens cap cover slips from my hand and plummets to the earth.

The ride comes to an unceremonious ending. The air inside the balloon gradually cools and we descend above a treeless plain. As the basket loses altitude, the pilot delivers a brief Balloon Landing Safety Orientation.

"For the love of God, say your prayers and hold on tight if you want to live," he says.

Actually, he doesn't say that, but he might as well have.

What he does say in a calm, even voice is, "I'll need you to crouch down inside your cubbyholes and take hold of the leather straps, please." Like it's no big deal.

I crouch down inside the cubbyhole and take hold of the leather straps firmly, and with both hands. The savanna rises up to meet us, and we come back down to earth harshly. Nearly all the tranquility we've stockpiled from floating above the Serengeti for the past hour is voided as the basket crashes into the ground. We hit at a high angle and catch, but the balloon continues flying. The momentum slams the basket over on its side and drags us through the tall prairie on our backs. I have a snake's-eye view of the terrain as the wicker steamroller careens across the prairie, firing on all cylinders. The basket shows no indications of slowing down, and dry straw and palm-size stones pelt me as they are scooped into my compartment. The pilot yanks on thick ropes to rein in the airborne bronco, but the basket mows down everything in its path, carving a neat scar across the plains. The balloon toys with us: It slows down and comes to a tentative stop, then jerks us another hundred yards. This is the last gasp; no longer able to keep herself aloft, the balloon slumps to the ground in a jumbled heap. The pilot gives us permission to de-balloon and we crawl out of our cubbyholes sideways, brushing loose grass off our clothes and fishing rocks out of our pockets.

According to the balloon company brochure, this kind of landing is "fun" and "boisterous."

A hundred yards away from the balloon's crumpled carcass sit five evenly spaced Land Rovers. Centered in front of the middle one is a table covered with silver ice buckets and bottles of fine champagne. In our haste to claim the bubbly reward, Tony, Selena and I dismiss the Deadly Poisonous Snake Safety Briefing from the hot air balloon pilot and hurry across the plains to the makeshift bar. A weathered steamer trunk sits in front of the table; inside, wooden boxes hold several dozen champagne glasses.

We soon learn that the highest concentration of Puff Adders and Black Mambas in all of Africa, if not the planet, is this stretch right here where the balloons landed and the champagne awaits, and we unknowingly skirted all of them. Chilled champagne in hand, we toast our snake-avoidance skills, as well as the green-and-khaki-striped balloon mounds slowly deflating behind us like enormous camouflage breast implants.

After a few glasses, we return the flutes to their boxes and climb aboard the matching Land Rovers. They chauffeur us down a narrow dirt strip to the breakfast site—stopping briefly to watch a pair of cheetahs wrestle—and soon arrive at a vast plain centered by a single red-thorn acacia tree. Impalas graze in the distance; a lone warthog scurries by. The nearest tree is almost half a mile away, so this one serves as an umbrella that provides shade for a long, cloth-covered dining table. A smaller table sits nearby, and a man wearing a white turban, an elaborate robe and a green vest that matches the tablecloths stands guard. He also wears a very serious expression; his lips are practically flat-lining. He holds a ceramic pitcher, and it appears that he is going to wash my hands.

This will be interesting: I've always washed my own hands, without assistance. I'll even dodge the bathroom attendant. But there is no getting around The Man in the White Turban, so I position my hands above a blue-rimmed bowl and hope for the best. He pours warm water over them, and for the first time in weeks, lavender-thyme soap from Great Britain replaces biodegradable camp suds. My hands will probably reject imported soap—and that will really annoy him—but they lather up just fine. He pours from another pitcher to rinse my soapy hands and hands me a fluffy towel without growing any sterner. All indications are that I have performed this correctly.

Relieved, I look for a tip jar. He doesn't have one, so I head to the dining table, which is set with fine china, silverware, a variety of glasses, linen napkins and additional silver buckets of champagne.

"Do you believe this?" asks Tony.

"This is the dog's bull-ooks," I say.

"Ball-ox," corrects Tony. "It's ball-ox."

"Pass me that champagne, will you?" says Selena.

A shamelessly decadent, ridiculously elegant breakfast begins, and additional turban-wearing, robe-bedecked men and women serve breakfast with formal style.

"We have definitely strayed into Abercrombie & Kent territory," I say, as a zebra with a remarkably full and lush tail runs by.

"I think we're acclimating quite nicely," says Tony.

"Do you think they might arrange a kill for us?" says Selena

"They probably have a robed man somewhere for that."

"Release the injured antelope," I say, holding a fist as a microphone. "Now cue the lion."

Hot egg dishes with bacon and potatoes appear out of nowhere, and waiters pour rivers of champagne, juice and coffee. The experience is all very sublime and ridiculous, and we cannot help but look at each other and laugh.

"I'm surprised they don't feed us," Tony says.

"Or wipe our mouths," I say.

"Do you think they'll make us flap?" he says, reaching for a cereal bowl.

"These people have definitely not been flapping," says Selena.

"Or crapping in holes."

"We should teach them," Tony says.

"Which one?"

"Do not flap," says Selena.

"I might have to," says Tony. "I'm addicted."

Breakfast ends and the group begins walking back to the Land Rovers. But wait—there is unfinished champagne here and we are not immune to its siren call. Tony, Selena and I linger at the table and, despite proper upbringings, check the proximity of turban-wearing authority figures before finishing off untouched champagne. Glasses are discreetly poured into ours and we quaff them down. This costs 300 shillings, and we are getting our money's worth.

Instant African karma gets me, and my favorite hat goes missing. The hat is floppy and khaki, the kind you'd attach lures to and go fishing in if you enjoyed that sort of thing. It is a solid companion and has risen in status from accessory to appendage. But as punishment for stealing champagne, it flies off my head and out the Land Rover's sunroof as we speed toward the Seronera Lodge. The champagne blunts my reaction time, and the belated grab is not even close. By the time the driver is notified, the AWOL hat is a quarter of a mile away, and he alerts the other jeeps via walkie-talkie. A professional rescue and recovery mission is under way, and the prized headwear is returned to me at the hotel. Whew.

Tony, Selena and I meet the rest of our group in the lobby and aim for humility and sobriety. Head-shaking, shoulder-shrugging speechlessness is my limited response to "How was the balloon ride?"

before managing a string of synonyms for amazing. Incredibly, the day improves.

Every 50 yards or so, hot *Animal Planet* action unfolds:

On the banks of a narrow river, three lionesses and a litter of young cubs explore the undergrowth and play atop a fallen tree trunk. A tight phalanx of elephants moves as one beside a dirt road. A dozen lionesses doze under a shady tree in a tangled orgy, with unclaimed paws poking up from between bodies. The first leopard of the trip barely camouflages himself in the tree branches as a dangling tail reveals his perch. A courting lion and lioness appraise each other between naps. There is one pool full of giant crocodiles, one with lazy hippos, and a third pool with cohabitating crocs and hippos. There are also more impalas, gazelles, giraffes, zebras, Cape buffaloes and waterbucks than we can really be bothered with.

A second leopard, this one with a kill, eats her lunch in the nook of a tree next to the road. From the balcony, the sleek cat is at eye level, and no more than 15 feet away. She could leap right over here if she wanted to. Instead, unnerved by the Bedford's size, she abandons the dead antelope and climbs down in front of the truck. She crosses the road, takes a perch in another tree and eyes her lunch. The group is overwhelmed by the variety of wildlife, and the proximity of the animals leaves us winded and satisfied.

Everyone, that is, but The Daft One.

He remains disinterested and unmoved. Ten feet from a tree-exiting leopard is simply not close enough to merit a photo or a memory.

"It was too far away," he grumbles.

The Bedford arrives at a dirt traffic circle carved out of thick acacia woodlands and parks beside several vans. The group disembarks only to find our progress halted by a spider the size of an elephant's foot. We gather around the massive arachnid, which freezes on the ground in a defensive position. When I kneel to take a photo, the enormous spider fills the frame of my zoom lens, and the fuzzy hairs that cover his body appear in microscopic detail. Objects in the viewfinder seem closer than they really are, so when the spider flinches one of his long, hairy legs he appears to lunge for my face and swat an eye out. I am up the stairs to the Bedford's balcony faster than a guy dodging a kamikaze bat.

"Look at him go," says Janet.

"That's the fastest The Yank's moved the entire trip," says Trevor, again.

We follow a path into thick underbrush and duck under branches lined with thorny spikes. The trail dead-ends at a steep slope that wraps around a watering hole. The tree-spotted crag is pimpled with large rocks, and several dozen tourists claim vantage points between the branches and well-positioned boulders. The scenic overlook is a precarious one because the pool beneath us is filled with crocodiles. Nearly a dozen of the thickly armored reptiles rest on the shore in the afternoon sun—who knows how many hide beneath the surface?

We are at least 30 feet above the water, and the hill is obstructed enough to prevent a crocodile from dashing up and snatching a tourist. But if a guest were to lose his balance or slip on a damp rock, or if someone were accidentally nudged off the trail, he or she could easily fall down the slope and topple into the crocodile pool. A person might not be able to escape from this side because the slope is so overgrown around the edges. The waterside trees would function as a lobster trap, allowing someone to slip through the branches and into the water but preventing an escape up the hill. Imagine the horror if a guest took a spill. Nobody would be able to rescue the person without putting himself in jeopardy.

On the opposite side of the tilted perch, The Daft One takes a rare interest in the wildlife and maneuvers around Roy for a clearer view. Perhaps he steps off the slick, narrow path and loses his footing, or maybe Roy accidentally bumps into him as they pass. The Daft One's left foot slips out from under him and his knee buckles. He grabs for a tree branch but it slides through his hands. His arms flail for balance and his leg crumples beneath him. The momentum carries him over and he lands on his head, cartwheeling down the hill in slow motion. Someone screams; it might be him. The Daft One plows into the thin stalks that grow along the shore and bend over the water's edge as if to drink. The boughs break, and the awful sound of snapping branches foreshadows The Daft One's plunge into the crocodile-infested watering hole. He folds up with the ease of a campfire chair, and his arms and legs scrape against the boughs as he splashes into the water.

The crocodiles sense the intrusion immediately and slide into the dark water to investigate. On the ravine above him, tourists watch helplessly as half a dozen rippled arrows streak toward a flailing bull's-eye. The hillside fills with shouts and gasps as The Daft One gropes for the shore and punches through the web of branches that holds him captive. He searches for an opening, but even the gap he created while falling in seems to have closed over. He spins around and watches the six snouts close in on him. An adrenalin surge courses through the man's veins and he wills himself out of the water, forcing his body into the tangled boughs. A large reptilian head launches out of the water and a toothy grin closes around his hips. The crocodile yanks him into the pool as a second croc latches onto a shoulder and across his chest. The Daft One will get a great close-up photograph of the wildlife now, if he hurries. Too late. The crocodiles spin in opposite directions and shear The Daft One in half. He disappears in a cannonball contest of exploding water, until only a few tattered pieces of clothing float on the surface.

That last part about The Daft One falling into the crocodile watering hole and being eaten alive did not happen, but as I watched him from across the way, the possibility that it *could* happen popped into my head for a second, and then the Larium took over. As punishment for stealing champagne and imagining the gruesome death of a travel companion, my favorite hat goes missing a second time. My reaction time is still stunted, and the hat flies off my head

153

and lands 100 yards behind the truck. I press the alarm button, and the Bedford comes to a tentative stop. I am sitting in the balcony, so it seems as though only three people are annoyed with me.

"Someone lose a hat?" Kinyua asks from the driver's window.

"Uh, yeah. It was mine," I say.

"Do you want to go back for it?" he says.

Do I want to go back for it?

"Is it really all that important?" someone asks. "I mean, it's just a hat."

Just a hat?

The hat has flown halfway around the world, passing through seven countries in the last month. It has survived hippo pods, the mighty Zambezi and international luggage transfers.

"Yeah, I'd like to go back for it."

Kinyua and Thomas debate as to whether a safe recovery mission can be executed. They are serious about people not leaving their vehicles out here, but the hat lands in plain sight and the Bedford reluctantly shifts into reverse. The saintly Thomas leaps off the truck to retrieve it, and the hat is passed up to me. Whew.

"I should attach it to my head with a tent stake," I say, and receive no argument.

This happens around the corner from where, in a few moments, we will have our close-up encounter with the tree-exiting leopard.

"You know, if you hadn't lost your hat we would have seen the leopard that much longer," Brian says later.

Ouch.

An umbrella thorn tree attacks me. As additional punishment for stealing champagne, imagining the death of a travel companion and cutting into people's leopard-viewing time, a two-inch-long spike stabs me in the eye. The Bedford is returning to the campsite at the end of our memorable day. The din of our conversations drowns out the lethal buzz as the truck pushes against a cluster of armed boughs, and dozens of sharp wooden spears scrape alongside the truck. The branches are pushed forward almost to the snapping point, then the barbed arrows clear the open windows and shoot their quills into the truck interior. My seat is at the front of the Bedford, so I am the first obstacle in the way. The spikes are stealthy and swift and offer no time to react. A needle-sharp jab strikes my eye; it feels as though I have been swatted by a one-clawed lion. I cover my face and double over.

"Bull-ooks!" I say.

"Ball-ox," Tony corrects.

There is much concern.

Judith manages to peel my hands away from my eye to assess the damage, but it is just the eyelid. No serious eye parts have been punctured. She suggests putting some lotion on the wounded eye skin, and when we return to camp, Judith rubs aloe balm on the injured eyelid with the soft tip of her index finger. The umbrella thorn tree is not so bad.

There is tension in the Serengeti tonight, a rumble in the jungle. It is not the usual tension. Sure, the impalas and gazelles are a little skittish about being on the predator menu again, but this friction arises when QE2 asks Roy to fetch her a sleeping pad.

"Which one is yours, Mum?" Roy asks from inside the Bedford.

"Oh dear, it doesn't matter," she says.

"Well, you don't want Steve's. His has shit all over it," Roy yells, leaning out the truck's window.

"Well, just hand me one that doesn't have a strong aroma, dear."

The hostility boils over in the dinner line when Roy threatens to impale The Daft One on the sharp end of his fork. QE2 misses all of today's spectacular sights and spends much of the day resting in her tent (when she isn't tidying the campground—even sick, this woman insists on doing her own flapping). Tonight, she and Roy will relocate to the Seronera Lodge so she gets a good night's sleep. Roy is *knarcky* about his poor mum and holds this man fully responsible. They have an exchange across the kitchen table while loading their plates with grilled chicken and roasted potatoes.

"So you think this is all my fault, do you?" asks The Daft One.

Roy's exact response is unintelligible, but his body language suggests that he says, "You miserable man. I would derive a great deal of satisfaction from inserting my kitchen utensil into your frontal lobe with considerable force." Roy jabs his fork toward the man's head for emphasis and huffs off. The Serengeti grows relatively quiet again.

DAY 12

The Serengeti to Ngorongoro Crater

As campsites are packed and chores completed, tension returns to Tanzania. A fight breaks out and results in a spinal injury. The conflict begins when a campfire chair insults Valerie, and she lashes out, kicking and pummeling the collapsible seat. Moments before the attack, I am helping her arrange the chairs inside their square cubbyhole. Everything seems to be going along fine, and there are no indications that Valerie is about to attack a chair. Quite the contrary, our chair-storage skills are improving daily, and they are going in with relative ease. Valerie takes charge and calls out instructions.

"Back-flap-side down, back-flap-side up."

"Back-flap-side down, back-flap-side up," I repeat.

Valerie is methodical yet calm as I flip the chairs around in the right direction and hand them to her. She stores the chairs inside the metal locker and pushes on them with all her weight to make more room. A pair of chairs is wedged in perpendicular to the stack, and our task is completed.

"Done," Valerie says in French.

We congratulate each other on a remarkable job as Marc walks around the corner with one more chair. Valerie snorts in disgust and kicks her foot in the dirt. The last chair becomes fractious immediately, and when Valerie pushes on the stubborn stool, it refuses to join its mates. She would have better luck coaxing a baby hippo in there.

"Why. Won't. You. Go. In?" she asks.

The chair's behavior does not sit well with Valerie, and she boils over with a measured fury. She appraises the seat with the laser focus of a lion about to attack, takes an authoritative step back and plants a foot solidly behind her. Then she erupts, landing a lethal blow against the defenseless chair.

"Whoa," I say.

A second assault launches from her angled torso and smashes inside the cubbyhole.

"Uh, Valerie . . ."

Her leg turns into an automatic battering ram as she lands repeated jabs. I do not recall this technique from the recent Campfire Chair Storage Seminar.

"Maybe Thomas can help."

She rears back, kicks her leg out and delivers another brutal chop. She attacks with precision accuracy, slamming the sole of her hiking boot into the chair's metal piping.

"We could just leave it."

There is some concern that Marc and I might have to restrain her. She is going to permanently damage the chair and make us accessories. I cock an eyebrow to ask Marc if this is new behavior, but he shoots me a "don't mess with her" expression. Valerie kickboxes the chair into submission and puts a terminal dent in its spine. The chair goes in, but it is never quite the same.

Our final Serengeti game drive begins and the Bedford retraces the route back to Ngorongoro Crater. After an hour, we have driven half a mile. First, we stop to watch the lion family from yesterday, the one that enjoys playing along the riverbank. Then we come across a lioness asleep under a tree. A few minutes later, another tree provides shade for a sleeping cat. In fact, almost every fifth tree has a napping feline beneath it. These sightings are the opposite of our first big-cat encounter, when the slightest lion movement left us unable to form complete sentences. By now, some of us have grown so desensitized to sleeping lions that we no longer lunge for photo equipment at the mere mention of one.

"Lion. Under that tree," Thomas reports.

"Bloody hell! A lion? Under a tree?" says Tony. "Scott, did you hear the news? There is a lion under a tree."

"A lion under a tree? You lie."

"I assure you. It's right there."

The presence of a large carnivore lying next to the road has grown so ordinary that the sight only moves us to sarcasm. It took less than a week.

"Is it . . . sleeping?"

"It does appear to be a little peaked."

Marc grabs his camera and narrates: *"Ici nous sommes dans le Serengeti et il y a un lion endormi sous un arbre."*

As usual, in French it sounds as though the lion is doing something spectacular, but she is only napping.

"I should get my camera. No one will believe this."

I snap a single photo. I'm turning into The Daft One. My portfolio of Sleeping Lions of Tanzania is added to, and the collection is huge.

A hundred yards up the road, a cheetah lies under a tree. A cheetah, even a sleeping one, I'll grab a camera for. A leopard sitting in a tree branch follows, then a stare-off with a trio of antsy hyenas hoarding bloody antelope parts. An animal that resembles a fox has us reaching for our guidebooks: It is a serval, a small cat with big ears and a reddish-yellow coat covered in large, black spots.

The best sighting of the trip happens when a cheetah comes skulking along the roadside. The group cannot believe it. A skulking cheetah! With acacia trees and rolling hills silhouetted behind her, the long-legged cat glides through the prairie, a whisper with spots. Behind her, the grass parts and a small cub emerges, followed by a second cub. It is a skulking cheetah mom. The mother cheetah looks back at her lagging brood and waits for the three of them to catch up with her. Triplets! The group is whipped up into a triplet-cheetah-cub frenzy, and the Bedford parallels the foursome across the Serengeti. Not far from the road, a termite mound pokes up from the landscape; it is a brown island in a sea of gold and lies directly in the path of the cheetah family. The group shares a similar thought:

"Wouldn't it be great if the cheetah mom climbed on the termite mound and stood there while the cubs played between her legs?"

The group agrees that those combined elements would indeed be quite splendid.

"That would be the dog's bull-ooks, for sure."

"Ball-ox," says Tony.

She does it. The cheetah mom climbs atop the termite mound and stands in the perfect light while the cubs play between her legs, snapping at each other's tails and generally romping around. The Bedford is rocked by a massive group climax. Even The Daft One acknowledges the significance of the moment by snapping two photos.

As if that weren't enough, a lion walks by. No shady tree for this cat; she walks across the savanna with decisive and evenly paced strides in the midday sun. The group cannot believe our good lion-hunting fortune. Another walking lion! The big cat is going somewhere, to do something, we speculate in hushed, earnest whispers. This rare behavior leads us to a single conclusion: She is hunting for lunch. Lion-induced euphoria erupts again as she cuts a path through the varied grasslands and disappears among the similar shades.

The truck's large windows offer a panoramic vantage point to search for the lion, and our elevated position reveals a small herd of gazelles directly in her path. If she continues in this direction, she will encounter the swift animals with the long, ringed horns as they graze

163

in a well-nibbled clearing. Surrounded by grassy knolls and elevated hiding places, the setting even resembles an arena, and the spectators are only waiting for the lion to be sent in.

Tension builds as the group waits for the cat to reappear from the grasslands. There she is: She emerges from a gulch and slips through the tall grass unnoticed. She is heading straight for the delicious animals, and they have no idea.

"Wouldn't it be lovely to see a kill?" says Selena.

Whether "lovely" is the best description for the carnage a lion will inflict on a helpless gazelle is debatable, but I'm all for it.

The lion moves between the truck and the herd and stalks them from behind a knobby ridge. Shutters click. Kodak stock skyrockets. People gape at one another in disbelief. A walking, stalking lion! She crouches in the grass and eyes the unsuspecting herd, providing us with front-row seats. The guests maneuver into position and wait for the ultimate safari sighting; I can barely keep my zoom lens from shaking. A crouching lion is about to pounce. The gazelles are oblivious to the stealthy cat, which is 20 yards away from a delicious meal. The daily struggle for survival unfolds on the plains of the Serengeti as the large predator crawls low in the grass and inches closer. This particular grass must be very soft and comfortable, because suddenly the cat lies down. She rests her head on her forepaws and takes a nap. She is, ultimately, another sleeping lion.

"It's time to go. OK? All right," says Kinyua.

"No. We can't go."

"She's got to eat."

"*Mais non!*"

The group turns into a truckload of adolescents who have just been told their field trip is over.

"No. We can't go."

"Just a few more minutes?"

"She likes gazelle."

"Wake up! Wake up!"

"*Mange! Mange!*"

The group is disconsolate about vacating potentially hot *Animal Planet* action, but a long drive lies ahead and we have a schedule to keep. As the Bedford exits the Serengeti, our farewell image is another lioness draped across the hump of a massive boulder, her head curled atop a furry paw. She sleeps.

Sarah has an evolved traveling skill. Just as the lion can fall asleep in the most unlikely position, Sarah can sleep aboard the Bedford while sitting upright. Her body gyrates wildly, but she remains in a deep slumber.

"Are you watching this?" I ask the group.

Her torso revolves in a wide circle as she swivels down an imaginary slalom course, and still she sleeps. The truck rolls over a pothole and her body pitches to one side, then heaves to the other.

"How can...how can she do this," I say, the laughs building.

Her head bangs with the ferocity of a heavy metal guitarist's and thrashes away to an unheard song. She is a rag marionette, flopping about in the hands of a drunken puppeteer, unrestricted by bones or a spinal cord. She teeters between human bookends, reeling into one person and head-butting another.

"This is . . . not . . . p-p-p-possible," I stammer, and dissolve into a heap of unintelligible huffing.

The more she bobs and weaves, the harder I laugh. My contortions are almost as comical as Sarah's: My shoulders quake and my stomach doubles over. My breathing becomes labored and tears stream down my cheeks. As usual, I continue to point out the obvious spectacle to the other guests.

"Are . . . you . . . you . . . wa-wa-watching this?"

But I can only point with a shaky wrist and make loud hiccup noises before grabbing my midsection. I am nearly helpless as she performs this spastic dance mile after mile. Abruptly, Sarah stops and wakes. She opens her eyes and sits up straight. She looks directly at my tear-stained face, unaware that she is the muse for my deluge.

"Scott, what's wrong?" she asks. "Why are you crying?"

"Be . . . be . . . because everyone's so . . . so nice," I manage, sobbing.

Within minutes, she is asleep again and continues her logic-defying slumber fit. At the onset of hyperventilating to death, I force myself to look at the scenery.

The Bedford arrives at Ngorongoro Crater, and our camp is set up along the southwestern rim, 2,000 feet above the crater floor. The self-contained ecosystem is one of the planet's greatest natural wonders and is essentially a zoo on the honor system, with more than 25,000 animals roaming around the golden, green-rimmed bowl. Because of the permanent water and pasture, the 100-square-mile conservation area has evolved into a tasty ruminant buffet for the lion prides that call the place home—and have it made.

The crater wall drops off right outside our tent doors and a natural fence of trees and thick undergrowth keeps us from tumbling in. The popular campsite is an outdoor gear showroom with at least 100 other tents scattered about a gently sloping lawn. Clusters of matching models are erected around a large flattop acacia tree, which manages to compete with the crater for Best Picture. There is not another tree nearby, so the lone trunk deftly centers the campground, and the fright wig of leafy branches explodes in a static electricity blast, except for the top, which appears to have been trimmed by an even hand. The ground slopes off behind the tree, so as the sun sets it is visible from trunk to top in a blazing silhouette. In the evening, the tree blends into the darkness, and the group gathers around the campfire for post-dinner cocktails and conversation.

Everyone, that is, but The Daft One.

He places his chair away from the other guests and leans against the Bedford's side, beneath a truck light.

"Be careful inside your tents," Kinyua says.

"Careful?" says Minouk. "Why do we have to be careful?"

"Oh, there are occasional robberies here."

"Robberies?" asks Minouk. "Oh no."

167

"Yes. They cut through people's tents at night," says Kinyua.

"Oh my gosh," continues Minouk. "How?"

"With a knife," says Kinyua.

"A knife!"

"They slit the tents open and reach inside and steal whatever they can. OK? All right."

"Wha—" says Minouk.

Abruptly, a portal of hell opens and *Hannibal* comes to life. A pack of giant forest hogs emerges from the darkness and appears behind our flimsy Maginot Line of campfire chairs. By the time someone says "Hey, look at those giant forest hogs," they are charging the campsite, and their monstrous breath practically tickles the backs of our legs. These pigs are identical to the ones I have been picturing in *Hannibal* for the past two weeks: massive, drooling beasts with coarse hair and severe tusks. The campfire throws menacing shadows against their jagged profiles, and their devil eyes glow red in the fire's reflection. They vacuum the ground like bad genetic accidents between warthogs and giant Hoovers, and surely my next adventure will be traveling through a pig colon. They take a sharp right when they reach the chairs and veer toward the Bedford, where a truck sconce highlights The Daft One. Per Satan's instructions, they close in on him, and I envision the man-eating pigs from the book dismembering their victims with brutal swiftness.

The Daft One is moments away from a porcine Cuisinart.

A split second from now the pigs will cover the distance to him, and their tusks will make contact with his pasty flesh. They will slice through tendons and bones and roust him from the chair, spilling him to the ground. The Daft One will fall prey to their ruthless appetites and disappear in a flurry of dark hair and kicking hooves and blood-soaked ivory.

But, unlike their literary counterparts and in spite of their ferocious demeanors, these pigs are a skittish bunch. That they are susceptible to a bit of yelling and frantic torch jostling is discovered just in time, and this knowledge emboldens us. The pigs spare The Daft One at the last moment and scavenge their way to the next campsite in a nightly hunt for leftovers. Beneath a hidden moon, we chase giant forest hogs around the campground above Ngorongoro Crater.

DAY 13

Ngorongoro Crater to Keratu

The sun hovers just beneath the skyline when I unzip the tent. The door flaps open, and a giant abyss is barely visible at the edge of the campground. The crater slowly fills with light, as if a heavy lid is being lifted from an oversize kettle. The light is filtered through a layer of mist that floats above the rim and is slowly erased by the sun. Several minutes pass before the entire crater is revealed, and each of them is sublime; I am humbled into dumbstruck reverence. The rest of the day should be good too. The group will abandon the Bedford for the first time and board small jeeps for a private tour inside the Eighth Wonder of the World.

As a kid I remember being glued to an episode of *Mutual of Omaha's Wild Kingdom* after a crater lion charged across the television screen and tackled a zebra. The lion brought down the sprinting blur in a cloud of dust and grass, and shushed her with a crimson bite. From that moment, I was hooked. This destination has sat atop my travel wish list ever since; being here is nothing short of childhood bloodlust come true.

The group buzzes around the campfire in the morning, eating breakfast and preparing for the long-awaited adventure. Most of the day will be spent on the crater floor, so we pack lunch bags for a mid-afternoon break. The guests circle the kitchen table and mimic hungry vultures, snatching fruit and grabbing for chocolate bars. As usual, I make a peanut butter and jelly sandwich, and much like my dirty pants, my reactions to bats and spiders, the way I pronounce "python" and "bollocks," and my general all-around Americanness, my PB&J intake continues to be mocked by the British.

"You're going to eat two of those?" asks Janet.

"Yes," I say.

"Didn't you have one for breakfast?" says Selena.

"Yes, but on toast."

"That is disgusting."

"No wonder we're out of peanut butter," says Tony.

"We're out of peanut butter?"

Fortunately, Tony is kidding; there is another jar. This peanut butter is not of the thickest consistency—it resembles some of the natural stuff—but the jelly is fine. Besides, it's tough to screw up a PB&J. Most of the Brits find the whole concept nasty and repulsive and quickly empty several tins of sardines instead.

"Yeah. Peanut butter and jelly is disgusting, but an anchovy sandwich? That'll hit the spot."

"They're really quite tasty," insists Janet. "You should have a go at it."

This from the people who brought you bangers and mash.

Several dozen Land Rovers with various outfitter names on their doors pull into the campground and park on the gravel road running along the perimeter. A herd of tourists exits their campsites and begins a human migration across the grassy field. Grabbing backpacks and lunch sacks, we split into small groups and head toward our cars. Each one holds only four passengers, so the night before—before the pigs attack—there is considerable jockeying for Land Rover position. Nobody wants to taint his or her experience in one of the most incredible places on the planet by spending eight hours in a Land Rover with a smelly guest, so alliances are formed and honored. Joining Tony and Selena is a given, and we suspect that our card-playing foursome will reunite. But Judith accepts a previous offer from Trevor and Brian to ride with them and Minouk. To Selena, this is nothing short of safari betrayal.

"Bloody hell. She can't ride with those blokes," she says. "Well, we're not riding with Steve, so hitch up with someone."

Two singles are available: Susan and Sarah. I still have only a moderate success rate with Susan's English, and she still seems mortified by our bathroom encounter, so I hitch up with Sarah; Valerie, Marc, and Susan ride with The Daft One. Our squad turns competitive the moment we climb inside with Simon, our driver: The other Land Rovers have to be outraced to the crater, particularly the one carrying Judith and the blokes. Simon, who looks sharp in a crisp green ranger uniform, is cheered as he outmaneuvers the other jeeps and speeds past them. He turns the road that borders Ngorongoro into his own racecourse and approaches the entrance in first place.

A glorified tollbooth adjacent to a small office marks the entrance to the crater, and a flimsy metal gate provides access to the

Eighth Wonder of the World. Our jeep arrives second, behind a Bedford-size camper van with German license plates.

"They're not going to go down in that, are they?" asks Selena.

"I don't think they can. They need a guide," I say.

"Simon, I thought only jeeps like yours were allowed in the crater," says Tony.

Simon looks at the huge RV with a perplexed brow and nods his head. Then a frumpy middle-aged woman storms out of the tiny check-in office, red-faced and fuming. She whips around and shakes a piece of paper at the official-looking men who trail her angry wake. She marches to the driver's door and shakes the paper at someone in the van's front seat. The woman's stout frame actually leaves the earth as she stomps the ground and kicks up clouds of dust. The door flings open and a barrel-chested man leaps out of the camper van. He snatches the paper from the outraged woman and now he shakes it at the unfazed officials. He appears to be saying "I have an important piece of paper here," but no amount of paper shaking sways the two rangers. They have rules here: Only authorized Land Rovers with certified guides are permitted in the crater, not oversize camper vans with Europeans on holiday. From inside our Land Rover, the confrontation plays out in pantomime, like a silent movie that has just stopped being funny. They return to the van and lock the doors. They roll up the windows, turn off the engine and sulk.

"What are they doing?" says Selena.

"Let's get a move-on, people," says Tony. "We have rhinos to see here."

"Are they just going to sit there?"

"They're blocking the crater," I say. "They're blocking Ngorongoro Crater."

Their rationale appears to be that if they are not allowed to take their big RV into the crater today, no one is going in, so on the morning of September 22, the main entrance to Ngorongoro Crater is blocked. By the time the couple begins sulking, half a dozen Land Rovers are parked behind us, wondering what the delay is and honking their horns loudly. As the two tourists hold the crater hostage, 50 more Land Rovers arrive on the access road. A traffic jam forms, and the passengers gradually emerge to see what the holdup is. A Felliniesque crowd of uniformed park rangers, assorted Land Rover drivers, tour guides, international tourists and curious, spear-wielding Maasai warriors surrounds the camper van, yelling and pleading with the couple in a variety of ineffective languages. At one point, Roy leads the charge.

"People are on vacation. This is the only day they have here and you are ruining it. Now move your bloody van," he says.

QE2 beams. Meanwhile, they sit inside the van, stoic and defiant. Precious minutes tick away, and I circle around to get a good look at these bozos. As I stand between the van and the gate, a few feet in front of their windshield, the woman initiates eye contact. She motions at me, grasping an imaginary pole with both hands and hoisting it toward her shoulders, as though she's doing invisible bicep curls. She wants me to lift the gate's metal bar so they can drive their van into the crater, and make me an accessory to Illegal Crater Entry.

I can't believe the gumption of these people and return to the solidarity of the crowd before they pull a *Dukes of Hazard* and ram through the gate like the General Lee.

"Maybe if we all heave together we can roll them into the crater," someone jokes to the crowd, but nobody takes me up on it.

Finally, a young man with a mop of curly hair says something succinct and persuasive in their native tongue, and the emasculated husband begrudgingly starts the engine and backs out of the way. The crowd returns to their Land Rovers, the drivers start their engines and the gates to Ngorongoro Crater open. Although our car is first in line, the RV blocks us when it backs up, and all the other Land Rovers drive by. Trevor, Brian, Judith and Minouk pass us, waving and laughing.

Simon snakes down the switchback trail that clings to the crater wall and winds to the floor. After maneuvering around a dead waterbuck—a large antelope with an ill-placed bull's-eye of white fur on its behind—the jeep arrives on the legendary plains of Ngorongoro Crater. We stand on the seats and poke our heads through the canopied sunroof, gazing up at the steep, rippled walls. A well-positioned cloud resembling a cat's head peers over the rim and furthers the illusion that we are at the bottom of a giant saucer. My initial impression is:

"Man, these jeeps are low."

"We might as well be walking," says Tony.

"How do people see from these things?" I wonder.

The strapping Bedford has spoiled us for anything less than a double-decker bus, where our elevation is so high, we can look a giraffe in the eye; in the balcony, we might as well be in a low flying airplane. But now our mortal Land Rover feels earthbound and claustrophobic. My second impression is that the crater is a drive through Eden. This is truly God's navel: a perfect ecosystem tucked away inside a massive stone innie. The setting is idyllic; the views are epic and stirring; the animals are beyond counting. And yet, our displays of awe and amazement are slightly tempered. Unfortunately, the group has reached that stage of the trip where our animal checklists overshadow the journey. We are a tough crowd, and Tony, Selena and I issue our specific requirements to the guide on the drive in.

"OK, Simon, here's what we're looking for today. We want lions. Lions eating. The food chain in action. No sleeping lions," I say. "We have seen enough sleeping lions."

"And Simon, we fancy a rare black rhino," Tony says.

"Yes, that would be lovely," says Selena. "A mother rhino with a baby."

A rhino sighting will complete our viewing of The Big Five (leopard, lion, elephant, buffalo and rhino), the universal benchmark of African wildlife scorekeeping, and the success of our day in the crater soon depends on a leathery beast with a big horn. Simon works hard to please us, but no amount of animals will do. He drives alongside Lake Magadi, whose shores are tinted with pink from the feathers of greater flamingos, distinguished from the lesser flamingos by their bright bills. The flamingos stop feeding and take off in unison, filling the sky with a ripped sheet of blushing ribbons.

"Some guy just pushed the 'flamingoes, flying' button," I say.

"Of course. There is a control tower up at the rim," says Tony. "Next, a pod of hippos will exhale at once."

Near the shore, mini geysers erupt from the water's surface, and a pod of hippos rises along the shore. Simon pulls up to an enormous herd of zebras. This is the largest amount of zebras any of us will ever see. The herd is a live Pollock painting, a hypnotic swash of black and white set against a backdrop of green and gold.

"Cue the zebras," I say.

But, our wonder and astonishment are diminished by the lack of a rhino trotting across the plains in front of them.

"Do you want to stop?" Simon says.

The group shrugs at one another.

"No, we've seen enough," Tony says.

"We've got to see a black rhino," Selena says.

The jeep maneuvers into an impromptu parking lot filled with two dozen identical Land Rovers all pointed at a lone male lion with his head inside a disemboweled Cape buffalo. This is potentially exciting, but the crowd of jeeps jockeying for position makes the experience resemble feeding time at Lion Country Safari, and we spur Simon on. He parks in front of a wildebeest mini migration: A thousand underfed, bearded cows roam the plains, walking around in a large, loose circle.

"Cue the wildebeests," I say.

"Perhaps they'll go counterclockwise today," Tony says.

"Do you want to stop?" asks Simon.

"Nah, keep going," I say.

"We've got to see a rare black rhino," Selena says.

The Land Rover parallels a zebra leading a large herd of wildebeests in a single-file line that zigzags across the crater floor.

"Do you want to stop?" Simon says.

"That's pretty cool. I'll take a shot of that," I say, and snap an obligatory series of photos so as not to offend.

Simon finds a den with a hyena family. A cursory glance is spared. A pride of lions sleeps on the grass; we have seen that before. Thousands of impalas, gazelles, zebras, giraffes, Cape buffaloes and waterbucks stand around waiting to be eaten.

"I'm going to be pissed if we don't see a bloody rhino," Selena says.

"Cue the rhino, Simon," suggests Tony.

Our single-focused enthusiasm becomes a germ that infects our judgment, a disease none of our trip inoculations provides immunity against. Rhino zeal becomes our sole source of motivation, and we grow increasingly fixated. If we do not see a rare black rhino, today will suck. We are turning into a jeep of Daft Ones. The man didn't just poison us with water but with his rotten attitude, and we are infected. No animal sighting is good enough. Simon shows us dozens of one animal, hundreds of another and a thousand of a third species. But we are here to see only one. Ngorongoro Crater is our best and last chance to see a rare black rhino.

"What do you think that is?" I say to the group, pointing to the intricate console above the stick shift. "Is that a rhino traffic controller or something?"

"Hmm, it does look like a rhino radar screen, doesn't it?"

"Fire that up, a dozen little rhino bleeps pop up on the screen. We drive right to them."

"Simon, what is that?" Tony asks.

Nearly a dozen rhinos live in the entire crater, and they are collared, tagged, numbered, monitored, named and horn-printed. The ranger only has to engage the console to pinpoint the whereabouts of each one.

"Does that tell you where the rhinos are?"

It does not. We meander around the crater floor and see everything but a rare black rhino. Sarah's head begins to bob again, and her chin bounces off her chest. She falls asleep in Ngorongoro Crater, but it is not nearly as funny as that time before.

Lunchtime arrives, and my priorities shift from tracking rhinos to eating peanut butter and jelly sandwiches. The enormity of eating a PB&J in Ngorongoro Crater does not go unnoticed. Africa and PB&Js are childhood signposts; I was probably eating one when I watched the lion tackle the zebra during that episode of *Mutual of Omaha's*

Wild Kingdom. My mom used to bring peanut butter to restaurants; I would go years eating nothing else.

The place where I'm going to eat the sandwich is a flat clearing that borders a small lake. Except for several hundred stampeding wildebeests, an elephant wading through the lake's vegetation and an antelope corpse floating in the water, this is Tanzania at its most theme park. A parking lot of nearly 50 jeeps forms next to the lake and hundreds of tourists gather on the grass. All that's missing is a T-shirt shack and a concession stand selling ostrich burgers and rhino mouse pads.

Circling above the lunchtime crowd is a squadron of yellow-billed black kites. The black kites, which are brown, are nimble and fearless divers of sandwiches, and can spin, detour and feed in midair. The agile daredevils orbit above us, monitoring the crowd for distracted diners and unattended meals. They find an opening, nose-dive into the crowd and snatch a sandwich or a slice of fruit that a tourist has set on the grass. One bird swoops down to a woman and snatches a piece of bread right out of her hands. She screams and flails, and we glance over to see a brown-winged flash and a forked tail escaping with a mouthful of food. The opportunistic kites are hungrier than a crowd of boys fighting over a pen and attack the successful bird until they rip the food out of its beak.

One can only imagine the prize a PB&J would be, especially these, and my sandwiches receive vigilant protection. They have been marinating in their own peanut butter and jelly juices in a Ziploc bag with the air sucked out for nearly three hours now. Properly aged, tightly sealed PB&Js take the PB&J eating experience to the next level; these will be transcendent. The sandwiches are pulled from their bag and are already discolored from the amount of toppings they've absorbed. The depth is a good half inch in some places; in others, the purple-and-brown smears permeate completely through the white bread. This melding creates lip-smacking nirvana that softens the bread and seals the ingredients into a congealed masterpiece. A PB&J is eaten in Ngorongoro Crater; I wouldn't trade it for a rare black rhino.

Toward the end of the day, departure time looms and rhino fanaticism peaks. Tony gives Simon a short list of demands.

"Simon," Tony says, "take us wherever we're most likely to see a rhino."

Simon circles back into the Lerai Forest, which forms a half-moon around Lake Magadi, the largest lake in the crater. We drive past clearings filled with antelope and under trees whose limbs are weighted with monkeys. A number of indifferent zebras graze close to a sleeping lion, and a leopard is barely camouflaged among the branches, but our horned friend remains truly hidden. Toward the end of the day, Simon notices a handful of jeeps congregating near one side of the crater wall.

"Sometimes a rhino is over there," he says, inspiring a burst of false hope.

He drives toward the other jeeps and pulls up alongside them. We gaze off in the direction of the other passengers and aim our binoculars toward the steep walls.

"Excuse me, what are you looking at?" I ask a passenger in the next jeep.

The passenger points to a lioness that is about three feet from the road, asleep.

Our day ends and Simon climbs the switchback trail that leads out of the crater. We depart the Eighth Wonder of the World slightly disappointed and grow resigned to a life without seeing a rhino in Ngorongoro Crater. If there is one spot on the planet where you are almost certain of a sighting, this is the place; the brochure practically guarantees it.

The Land Rover returns us to the campsite where Brian celebrated his birthday, God spoke to me and we discovered that The Daft One made us all sick. Our tents are already set up. The sight of two perfect rows of neatly spaced tents welcomes us as we pull in. Saint Thomas has done this, elevating his status to the blessed. Everyone is worn out from driving around all day, and not having to put up our tents is a slight rhino consolation.

DAY 14

Keratu to Kilimanjaro

Not that much happens today. Valerie and I can finally store the chairs without kicking or supervision; that's progress. Chair storage seems fairly remedial now, and we are stumped to explain why it confounded us. I flip the chairs around in the right order and she stores them inside the metal locker. Done. I've also gone three days without a delusion; another milestone.

The campsite is packed, and the Bedford begins the long drive across northern-central Tanzania, from Ngorongoro Crater to Mt. Kilimanjaro. The group spends almost the entire day aboard the truck playing cards, watching the scenery, reading and sleeping. Our trip is nearly over, and everyone is worn out. We don't even wave to the locals with the same enthusiasm; it's almost perfunctory.

The Bedford follows the road to Lake Manyara and heads down the eastern slope of the Rift Valley Ridge toward the T-shirt shop with the nice bathrooms, where QE2 gave out her pens.

"This is the first place I threw up," Valerie says.

Ah, memories. Since the T-shirt shop proprietor allowed us to sully his fine flush toilets on the way in, we compensate by purchasing large amounts of souvenirs and blankets. The Bedford continues west, and Tim and I can successfully count to ten.

"*Mo-jaw, mbee-lee, ta-too, naw-nee, taw-noh, see-taw, saw-baw, naw-nay, tee-saw, koo-mee.*"

We stop near the campground where almost everyone became sick, at a marketplace with a dirt courtyard ringed by cramped aluminum stalls. Climbing off the truck is like walking into an unorganized audition for *The Lion King*, and we push our way through a crowd of masks, animal carvings, *shulas* and batik mosaics. The shopkeepers herd us into stall after stall of identical goods, and assure us that they are our friends and have special prices especially for us.

"How much do you want to pay?" they ask, whenever we look interested in an item.

Many of the stalls have various carvings of The Big Five (an elephant, a leopard, a lion, a Cape buffalo and a rhino) sitting around a table drinking beer. Hanging from a nail in one stall is a necklace with a stone pendant and a painting of a giraffe that my sister, the big giraffe fan, would like.

"How much is this?" I ask the storekeeper.

"How much do you want to pay?" he says helpfully.

I do not want to pay a lot for this giraffe necklace, but a number is tossed out to keep the experience going. My offer is very upsetting to the man and causes him to shake his head and grab his stomach. But because he is a reasonable businessman, he recovers quickly and counters with a number a lot higher than my original offer. Haggling is not my strong suit; I wish the stuff just had price tags. The vendor is dismissed without a follow-up offer, and I wander off into a neighboring stall. This guy has the exact same carvings of African wildlife enjoying a lager—"The Big Five Drinking Beer" in wood seems to be the Tanzanian equivalent of "Dogs Playing Poker" in velvet—but no giraffe necklaces.

Looking up, I see The Giraffe Man standing outside the stall, taunting me. He holds the giraffe pendant out to me and swings the pendant from side to side, slowly. My gaze quickly diverts to a lion sharing a beer with a rhino. The store has no back exit, so I walk right past The Giraffe Man, who follows me, assuring me that we are close, personal friends and he has a special price especially for me. Every few minutes I see him standing outside whatever stall I am in. He swings the pendant from side to side, slowly, back and forth, as though he is trying to hypnotize me.

Before walking out of here with armloads of giraffe knickknacks, I return to the Bedford, which continues east and heads for Arusha's more modern downtown district, away from the bars, the lumberyards and the clusters of La-Z-Boys. The streets are lined with clothes stores, markets, banks and money exchanges. Most of the group settles in an Internet cafe for a snack, and I let my friends back home know that I am still alive and have not succumbed to any animal bites, fatal diseases or giraffe necklace hypnosis.

The Bedford begins the final leg of the trip to Marangu, a town on the southeastern slopes of Mt. Kilimanjaro. Our tents sprout on the grounds of a sprawling Victorian hotel set against a backdrop of green trees, hedges and multitiered lawns. We have showers, flush toilets, a bar with outdoor seating, even a swimming pool. The skies are overcast, so our only views of Mt. Kilimanjaro come from the labels of Kilimanjaro Beer.

DAY 15

Kilimanjaro

Mt. Kilimanjaro is the largest of nearly 20 volcanoes that stretch across the East African Rift Valley. Africa's tallest peak is 19,336 feet tall and the highest freestanding mountain in the world. The conical volcano erupts from the ground as dramatically as that thing beneath Trevor's eyebrow and towers above the surrounding plains. The Maasai people named her *Oldoinyo Oibor,* which means "white mountain," because a crown of snow nearly always tops the summit's lunar landscape.

The group climbs into the foothills of Kilimanjaro, except for The Daft One. Trevor and Brian stay behind too, and are still in their sleeping bags as we head down the hotel's long driveway. The rest of us accompany a local guide and hike the cultivated farmlands and lush rain forests that cover the lower slopes. The rumpled valleys are carpeted in a sheet of green shades and produce so much oxygen that taking a deep breath is almost intoxicating. The pure air is a natural narcotic, and my lungs tingle and stretch trying to gorge themselves on the new taste: refreshing oxygen scented with banana trees and flowering vines. Somebody should bottle this stuff.

Even more impressive than the fresh air is the fact that we are standing at the base of a nearly 20,000-foot mountain. The peak shoots out of nowhere, in absolute isolation, sheer from the flat plains.

It is right there, towering above us. At least, that is what we are told whenever we ask where Mt. Kilimanjaro is.

"It's right there," our local guide says, pointing to the thick cloud bank that hangs in front of us like an impenetrable curtain. "It's right there."

Kilimanjaro. Rhino. Things we do not see in Tanzania that end in an *o*.

While hiking the well-trod paths that crisscross Kilimanjaro's rolling suburbs, a vague hum drifts in and out of earshot, faint and unidentifiable. The muted notes roll down from the hills and disappear into the treetops. As the group climbs higher, the terrain creates a natural amphitheater for the slight melodies, and they emerge clear and fully formed.

Church choirs are singing.

Today is Sunday, and the local congregations are full. The voices provide a gospel soundtrack for our walk in the woods, and a dirt path feels as sacred as a cathedral aisle. We follow one hymn down a dirt road bordered by thick trees and narrow driveways that lead to hidden wooden homes. The song grows louder and more urgent, and we arrive at the source: the front door of a concrete brick church.

The single-room structure has a white steeple roof supported by poles, and open windows with empty panes. The singers are mostly children and young teens, and their clothes are their Sunday best. A young girl of about 9 walks by in a shimmering, lacy dress and carries it with grace and perfect posture. A toddler brother clutches her hand, and she guides him toward the church door and the unwieldy steps. He teeters a bit pulling his second foot toward the top, but the older sister steadies his back and lifts him up.

We stand at the door and sneak awkward glances inside until Kinyua gives us permission to enter. We follow behind the two siblings and sit on narrow wooden benches in the back. A motley group of a dozen tourists cannot slip into the back of a crowded African church unnoticed, and each pew of worshipers slowly becomes aware of us. They swivel around until the entire congregation is staring at us. Their eyes are turned our way, but they are not unwelcoming. A young charismatic minister preaches in Swahili before interrupting his sermon to greet us.

"*Jambo, jambo,*" he says enthusiastically. "Welcome to Tanzania."

When the congregation begins the next hymn, they face away from the altar and sing to us.

The massive head of a painted lion squeezes between a pair of yellow shuttered windows and glowers from a cement wall. The ABCs, complete with accompanying illustrations for each letter (*E* for elephant, *G* for giraffe), stretch across an adjacent building. In spite of the adolescent artwork, the murals cover two wings of a vocational school perched on the side of a green slope. College-age students are learning various craft skills, and they lead us through classrooms filled with sturdy armoires, bright batiks and animal carvings. Delayed giraffe hypnosis strikes, and my sister gets a carving.

The group hikes alongside swift streams and through a vine-strewn jungle that spills into a miniature valley. A large one-room schoolhouse appears in a clearing and is hemmed in by a compact range of rounded hills. A wide lawn that doubles as an athletic field is the school's front yard, and a few boys kick around a soccer ball. Inside, the room is sectioned off into various reading nooks by large shelves lined with books and animated Disney videos. The school is tidy and well-cared for, and the walls are papered in colorful student drawings.

This school is the final destination for my treasure trove of pens; it is the culmination of their long journey. They will find homes here in the small hands of hardworking students. The pens will be prized possessions—beloved, even. I can see the kids now, holding them up to the sun and studying their curious mechanics, taking them apart, losing them.

My backpack is eased off a shoulder and placed on the floor, next to a shelf of children's books. A side pocket is unzipped and the corner of an envelope pokes out. I retrieve the envelope and pour out a handful of futuristic pens into my hand. The pens go flying, spilling to the floor and sending loose caps everywhere. They splatter across the room, and every conversation stops to see what the ruckus is—oh, it's just The Yank. Crawling around on my hands and knees, I scoop up the caps and match the colored tops with their partners. I hold the pens in my hand one last time and contemplate their long journey here. They have crossed an ocean, a sea and three continents in the last 20 days. The pens have survived hippo pods, the mighty Zambezi and international luggage transfers. They have driven across Tanzania without being tossed to a kid who probably doesn't even go to school. I clutch them and walk purposely toward the teacher. This is it, the Giving of the Pens.

"Hey, these are for the kids," I say.

I hand the pens to the teacher—a middle-aged British woman who walks five miles of twisting valley paths to school each day—who collects them in mid grasp.

"Oh, thank you," she says. "That's lovely. Thank you."

She slips the pens into the pocket of a smock and returns to her conversation, and that's it. The end. No child wriggles in anticipation at the thought of a pen. No kid lights up at the receipt of a foreign Bic. Nobody gazes up at me in slack-jawed wonder and silently lionizes me as The Great White God of Writing Utensils. Nobody has a pen snatched out of his hands by a larger, bullying kid. There's no fighting, no punching. The whole experience is gratification-free. The pens will probably sit in the teacher's pocket until they are tossed in a drawer with other anonymous pens.

The anticlimax of my small gesture is unsatisfying and I walk away, crestfallen. Next time, I'm bringing more pens and tossing them out by the handful, whether or not the kids are honor students.

I exit the classroom and walk across the cement veranda that overlooks the athletic field. More kids are outside, kicking a soccer ball or gathered on the stairs. The kids have a tape of a recent World Cup soccer match and are waiting for us to leave so they can watch the game on the school's VCR. Chances are, some of these kids will be on the receiving end of my cargo of pens. I should probably stop and tell the kids that the cool-looking pens are from me—the brightly colored ones that are sort of see-through and futuristic. Instead, I say *jambo* and continue down the stairs, parting the crowd and heading away from the school. A dirt path parallels the classroom windows and disappears behind the building. Rounding the corner, I nearly run over a 6- or 7-year-old boy holding a flower. The boy is a modern-day Gainsborough, dressed in a blue baseball cap, blue cords, a light blue T-shirt that pokes out from beneath a blue pin-striped oxford and a dark blue sweatshirt. I have startled the shy kid, who stands frozen on the grass.

"Jambo," I say.

I continue down a path that leads into a thick, green hillside to catch up with the rest of the group but haven't gone more than a few strides when I sense it. There is something in my pocket, the front right pocket. It feels like a pen. I reach my hand inside to make certain. It is. There is a pen left. I have a pen. Turning around, I walk purposely back to the kid and lean down to his level.

"Would you like a pen?" I say.

He does not respond at first. He is speechless, or does not speak English. He watches as my hand reaches into the pocket and inhales when he recognizes the sleek futuristic beauty of the pen, the pen that will soon be his. His eyes grow wide and he nods yes, yes, yes, swiveling his head around to see if anyone is witness to his great fortune or is about to beat the crap out of him. I hold out the pen to him, as though it contains a lifesaving vaccine, and with the impact of Mean Joe Greene tossing a sweaty jersey to a small child, I give the kid the pen. It's blue, of course. A blue pen for a blue boy. He clutches it to his chest and swoons. The kid leaps skyward and spins around. His reaction fills me with warm, international pen joy: two different cultures bonded by ink from Walgreens, just $1.29 a dozen. He looks at me with an expression both wordless and clear. You are a balding deity, it says. In the foothills of Kilimanjaro, in the hands of a small kid clutching a pen, I am, finally, a god.

I'm lying like a cheetah in the sun. A chronic-fatigued cheetah that just ate in the midday sun. The kid does not do any of that. That's what he was supposed to do, of course—the anticipated reaction. But the kid is unmoved by the awesome Pen From America and cares not that it crossed an ocean, a sea and three continents, or that it paddled around hippos and drove across Tanzania, or that I was recently chased by a bat. There's no leaping skyward, no international pen joy. I'm not God. The pen is not even blue—it's green. Except for the part where I hand the kid the pen, it is just a sad tale. Leave it to me to find the only child in all of Africa who does not want a cool pen from the

U.S. of A. No kid has ever wanted a pen less than this one; I practically have to force it into the kid's hand.

"Take the pen, kid," I practically have to say, "I'm giving you a pen, OK? Take the pen."

He does not seem all that certain as to what he might do with such a thing, frankly. No pressing correspondence, no urgent doodling. He studies the pen for a moment.

"*Asante, asante*," he finally says, which is probably Swahili for, "I hate green," or something.

The hike highlight is stopping at a hillside bar for Kilimanjaro's local beverage, banana beer. Boy, could I use one. The bar is a clapboard house tucked behind a fortress of banana trees and is dubbed Watcha's Banana Beer Bar after the woman who lives here. The bar is empty except for us, and we sit outside on wobbly stools beneath a large wooden eave. A chicken from next door pokes her head between a hole in the fence to see who's there while Watcha delivers a pitcher of banana beer to the thirsty hikers.

The beer is made from a centuries-old recipe blending bananas and millet, a fast-growing grain. The fruity malt takes a day to brew and arrives in a plastic bucket, the kind a kid might use to build a sand castle. This bucket looks as though a kid recently used it to build a castle and forgot to clean it. A boggy layer nearly an inch thick floats on top of the concoction. The head is not foam but a layer of leftover millet. Everybody looks at it skeptically, so I volunteer to take the first sip. It is beer, after all. A milk mustache the color of grain and the consistency of wet sand coats my face and drips down my lips. Something solid and earthy sticks between my teeth.

"It's a little thick," I report.

After passing the bucket, we ask Watcha for a sieve. She rolls her eyes at the tourists but brings a spoon, and we ladle out most of the solid parts. The drink doesn't taste much better, but it does resemble beer more. Watcha brings out a few bottles of banana wine for us to try. Banana wine is what banana beer should be: alcohol without the thick pieces.

Outside of Watcha's, an ancient gentleman walks by in a natty yellow blazer and a brown derby and shakes each of our hands. We follow him down a dirt thoroughfare that takes us through thick jungle and winding valleys, and we begin the final leg back to the Bedford. We have a pied-piper effect on the local kids, who chase after us and peer from between banana tree leaves and flowering plants. The kids hurry to the edge of driveways, brothers and sisters holding hands, smiling and waving and never asking for pens.

The man in the brown derby leads us to an entire banana beer bar district. On either side of the road are wooden houses filled with locals quaffing down banana beer. Watcha's place is not the most popular spot in Marangu, and these places are crowded and loud on what must be a Sunday afternoon post-church ritual.

A group of elderly women, swathed in colorful robes, sit outside of one bar on the grass. They are laughing and looped, downing bucket after bucket of banana beer. Each woman has her own ornamental mini sieve, and they carefully sift out the layer of sediment. I feel an immediate kinship with the women. They don't like leftover millet in their beer any more than the white folks.

Tonight is our farewell dinner at the hotel's large restaurant. The space sprawls across three hardwood-floored rooms and becomes crowded over the course of the meal. We scatter around a long table that takes up an entire room, and Kinyua delivers a toast.

"Well, I just want to say thank you. This was a great trip and a great group. And it was great that everybody got along so great. OK? All right."

What trip was he on? I wonder and share perplexed shrugs with the people at the other end of the table. For dinner, large plates are passed around family-style, and the drinks flow. Between the main course and the all-you-can-eat dessert buffet, a power surge or electrical failure knocks out the hotel lights and pitches the restaurant into complete darkness. For unexplainable reasons, this incites our table to launch into an impromptu variety of wildlife calls. We turn into a growling, howling, honking, hooting, yowling, woofing, baying, bleating, snarling, snorting, roaring mob. We are animals. When the lights come back on, the group stops barking and returns to normal. Our endless wit is directed toward an American tourist who repeatedly visits the dessert buffet table for more pie.

"Hasn't she already had a piece?" asks Selena, as the woman returns for another slice.

"This is her third," says Judith.

"We better hurry. There won't be any left," says Tony.

"Where does she put it?" says Selena.

"Did you get a look at her bum?" says Janet. "That's where."

"Scott, what is it with you people and pie?" asks Tony.

"What can I say? We're Americans, and we love our pie."

By the time the woman returns for a fourth slice, Kinyua excuses himself. Not even his sturdy constitution can withstand untreated drinking water, and he is the final casualty of our undiscriminating bug. He has hidden his illness from us the last few days but surrenders at the end and exits unceremoniously.

Most of the group retires to the hotel bar for our final evening together. Proving our unlimited capacity for tolerance and compassion, we invite The Daft One to join us, but he declines and sits by himself at a nearby table. Later, we migrate into a larger room, which is filled with chairs, couches and dozens of oddly shaped footstools that double as drums. The drums are true skins, tightly covered in impala and antelope pelts, but no endangered species. Before long, everybody is paired off with his or her own, and we pound away in an experimental drum circle. The impromptu jam session binds us in a new circle, a tighter one. After all the crap we have been through, we are finally a band.

A round footstool the size of a large zebra inspires a musical contest, and our final evening is capped with that concert staple, the drum solo. The footstool is passed around from person to person, and we pound the drum with our hands, our elbows, even our heads. One by one, the guests attack the stretched-out zebra skin with an animal fury, and we cheer each other's performances.

Tim drums like an athlete. He unleashes his lanky body and smacks the drum as though dribbling a basketball up and down a court.

Janet's brashness and energy course through her arms, and her drumming is as spirited as her personality.

Minouk lets her hair down, and freshly scrubbed locks replace the black ponytail. They cascade down her shoulders, blending into the zebra fur and bouncing off the footstool.

I don't know what I'm doing. I just start banging away until it sounds like a drum roll, then finish with a big, silly crescendo.

Sarah giggles and blushes as soon as she starts playing, and the crowd is still applauding as she pushes the drum kit over to Selena.

The zebra doesn't stand a chance: Selena's rock hard biceps flex and tense as she batters the pelt into submission.

Tony should have a cigarette in his mouth; he looks like he's in a nightclub.

Marc and Valerie drum in French, and Brian knocks out a sturdy rhythm that shakes the walls. Fittingly, Trevor is last. No one could have followed his performance. He is John Bonham reincarnate. He explodes over the drums and hammers away like Sarah sleeps: His head bangs; his body gyrates and his arms disappear in a blur.

Our cheers leave no doubt that Trevor beats all.

DAY 16

Kilimanjaro to Nairobi, Kenya

This is it. Our temporary family begins to separate. Tony and Selena, along with QE2, Roy, Susan and The Daft One, will continue with the guides to the Spice Islands of Zanzibar, while the rest of us begin the long journey home. Roy and The Daft One have another week of potential fork-impaling together. The shuttle is an hour late, so we pace around the Bedford and relax atop the small mountain of sleeping bags and duffels.

Tony, Tim and I kick a hacky sack around. QE2 does some last-minute flapping. The cloud situation is monitored in case Mt. Kilimanjaro treats us to a final glimpse before our exit, but she does not.

The guides pose behind the truck and we snap away as eagerly as fans at a movie premiere. Two neighboring campers are talked into taking a group photo, and we drape no less than 16 different cameras around their necks. We exchange e-mail addresses and promise to write, send pictures and plan future holidays together. The prolonged goodbye is awkward, and we hold off on any final farewells until the bus pulls into the hotel's campsite.

"Well, it was the dog's ball-ox," I say.

"Ball-ox! You can be taught," says Tony.

"Yes. It was lovely," says Selena.

Scott Balows

"Well, you've got to come to London," says Tony.

"And you to Chicago. We'll have deep-dish pizza," I say.

I bow to QE2, who calls me a dear boy. The group hugs and kisses both cheeks, these being Europeans and all. Everyone, that is, but The Daft One. He spends the entire morning sitting in a chair beneath a tree, unmoving and mute. As usual, he fails to engage the common reality. He nods at us absentmindedly as our bus pulls away, as though he will not miss us at all.

The journey home requires a nine-hour drive backtracking our way to the airport in Nairobi, followed by an equally long midnight flight to Amsterdam. The shuttle bus takes us to the hotel in Arusha, the one with the fenced-in parking lot, and we stock up on crackers and sodas. We move to a smaller van with just enough seats to hold the remaining members of our group and stay together until the end.

During the drive from Kilimanjaro to this hotel, I start to not feel so good. And not just because the trip is over, but as though I'm going to hurl. A sudden queasiness fills my stomach, and the taint of bile creeps up my throat. When nausea looms, my body notifies me by producing unimaginable—oh, you know what happens. Immediate precautions are taken. I chew some Pepto caplets and drink some water. The surrounding area is evaluated and the nearest exits are established. The window, which pushes out, is opened to see if my head can squeeze through there. It's a little tight; that could be a tricky maneuver. The van's sliding door can be opened quickly,

202

although I will need to factor in some time to ask the driver to slow down first. An empty plastic shopping bag sits on the floor between my legs and appears to be of sturdy construction. I think I can hurl with as little mess and spectacle as possible.

That I should be sick leaving Tanzania is the perfect ending—a mirror image to the opening salvo of the woman in her bathroom at the Hotel Boulevard, clinging to the toilet, nauseous. The glands run steadily, and the water bottle must be used for a spittoon all the way to Kenya.

At the border, the van stops so we can have our passports checked. A makeshift town has sprung up around the immigration offices, bordered by two facing rows of tin-roof stores and flimsy stalls lined with souvenirs, bars and money changers. Our driver tells us not to buy any souvenirs here. Not to visit the bars. Not to exchange our money. Instead, he herds us into the offices to have our paperwork shuffled and stamped. Since I am the first one out the door, my travel documents are processed before the others, and I return to the van to stand guard. I am woozy and light-headed, so any security will be mostly decorative.

Suddenly, a dozen Maasai women materialize across the road and spot me standing alone by the van door, as vulnerable as an antelope with a sprained ankle. They sense my weakness and break into a dead sprint, charging across the road in a bright swirl. The Maasai Olympics unfold, and the traditionally dressed women dash across the highway, their *shulas* fluttering behind them like giant plaid butterfly wings. The old ladies are deceptively fast and cover the distance between us in a few seconds. They have a dizzying variety of jewelry, spears, carvings and earlobes and thrust all of them into my face.

"No. No, thank you," I say. "Yes, they're nice. I just brought a giraffe."

My field of vision narrows and fills with earlobes. Large dangling earlobes children could swing from. Huge elastic ears, split in half, knotted up in bow ties. Stretched-out, hole-punched earlobes flapping around like small birds. A massive bout of Instantaneous Phantom Ear Pain strikes and I grab my own lobe. In the commotion, actual contact is made with a large Maasai lobe. The ear brushes against the back of my hand as I reach for the door handle.

What happens next is a bad dream. A rumbling begins in the cellar of my stomach and a churning swell floods my gut. I back away from the women, but that only draws them closer. I grab my stomach. Hunched over, under the noonday sun and the curious expressions of a dozen Maasai women, at the border of Kenya and Tanzania, I return the contents of my stomach to the African pavement in the great circle of life. The startled women leap backward in unison and emit surprisingly high-pitched shrieks. I do my best Victoria Falls impersonation, and a thick, muddy torrent gushes from my contorted figure, splattering a *shula*. My stomach empties and I lean over the soiled parking lot, hacking and spitting.

Someone places a hand on my shoulder, and a bright red blanket falls across my upper arm. I squint up at a Maasai woman; I can't really see her—she is silhouetted against the sun—but she pats my back in a universal gesture of hurling sympathy. I apologize to the women and climb inside the van while they search for healthier prospects.

The great thing about taking a four-week vacation is that after the four weeks I'm ready to go home. I'll spend a few days in Amsterdam, so while not exactly home, the city is a solid reentry into flush-toilet land and drinkable tap water. On shorter trips, I always wish I had stayed longer, thinking that a few extra days on a river or a trail would be the antidote to the habits of home. But not when I'm gone for a month. That's my limit, anyway. Stick a tusk in me; I'm done.

Driving across Kenya, I feel as though an umbrella thorn tree poked me in the eye and a vein is bleeding out. I am just kind of numb and lifeless. A fleece jacket folds into a pillow, and the van's vibrating door doubles as a mattress. Lulled by the rhythmic, steady driving on paved roads, I drift off. Moments and images replay—a highlight reel of funny exchanges and wildlife, of the magical and the mundane, of safety orientations.

A length of dental floss doubles as a clothesline. We reenact Monty Python sketches. A young zebra nurses from her mother. Peter delivers the Hippo Safety Orientation. My belt goes missing. A blue-balled monkey resists dashing off with a roll of matching blue toilet paper. Kinyua delivers The Tanzanian Explorer Orientation. A man tries to sell me a three-week-old *USA Today*. An ailing lion sports a back full of fresh scars. An old rogue male elephant with chipped tusks paces alongside the Bedford. We pay special attention to The Bush Camp Hole Orientation. Complete Cape buffalo skeletons, baked white by the sun, dot the plains. A Maasai warrior rides an old bicycle around the bush camp. Kinyua delivers The Serengeti Safety Orientation. A monkey incites a commotion when he launches himself toward the group, leaping from van roof to van roof and atop the Bedford. The hot air balloon pilot delivers the Balloon Landing Safety Orientation. Howls of laughter in a variety of British accents fill the Bedford. A kid holds a pen under duress. Kinyua gives The Campfire Chair Storage Orientation—wait, that was a seminar.

Our group has a smaller farewell dinner back at the Hotel Boulevard. We gather on a terrace next to the highway and listen to Nairobi's traffic hurtle by. My nausea retreats once I shovel some food in me, and I start to feel human again. After dinner, our band continues to break up; Sarah and Minouk are staying in Nairobi a few extra days, and we have another receiving line in the parking lot to say goodbye. At the airport, the rest of the group gathers in a bar for a final drink. The ending is anticlimactic. We toast our great adventure and then it's over. We go our separate ways. To England, Canada and America, to regular lives and familiar routines. Marc and Valerie are on my flight and will spend a few hours with me in Amsterdam, where more wild life awaits. But that's another tale.

The End.

Afterword

There is a rare black rhino in my kitchen. He stares ahead, unmoving and indignant, and looks at me from the corner of his eye. He pities me. Of course, this rhino is a wooden magnet, but the long horn juts out from the refrigerator door just the same, and the sunken eyes are no less judgmental. The animal is perched at eye level between a miniature row of San Francisco's painted ladies and a small Statue of Liberty. The endangered magnetized rhino is the first thing I notice upon opening the refrigerator to see what's to eat in there, which isn't much. This particular rhino actually came from Africa; two friends who traveled to Tanzania several years prior contributed the piece to my souvenir magnet collection. Now the rare black rhino mocks me for traveling halfway around the world when he was here all along. As I grab a beverage (my beer allegiance returns to refreshing, ice-cold Budweiser) and consider the miniature rhino facsimile, I have a single thought: I'll get you one day.

I meet with the Chicago Gang and the other friends who received the condensed, e-mailed version of this tale. Their first response is always, "That sounded like a wild trip," followed by, "What was up with that one guy?" That answer is as elusive as the rare black rhino. But letting The Daft One be the lasting impression of this tale won't do, even if he did provide the lion's share of the funny material.

The ending wants for an alternative wrap-up, so the memory vaults are searched for a nugget of Swahili wisdom. What is the moral here? What have we learned?

Monkeys like mangoes.

To a croc, your craft looks just like a dead, floating hippo.

Hippos can jump to their feet rather quickly.

The spinning dirt cyclone discriminates against no man.

The limping Cape buffalo will not see the dawn.

You can hurl a lot more than you think you can.

British accents are funny.

The dung beetle will never go hungry.

Don't drink the water.

Spend the extra bucks: Go with Abercrombie & Kent.

Once you've seen a sleeping lion, you've seen them all.

The animals will not break into song; the warthogs do not make wisecracks.

Sometimes, the easiest tasks aren't.

Britain and America really are two countries separated by a common language.

Bats, pigs and spiders are a lot scarier than crocodiles, hippos and lions.

I can survive without my Leatherman.

Not every kid wants a pen.

How about: You can still have a solid vacation if you're nauseous and diarrheic as long as you have a healthy sense of humor?

That laughter truly is the best medicine? Unless you're really sick or bleeding; then you should see a doctor for sure.

It's been six weeks since I left Africa, and I am heading to the U.K. for a mini-reunion. Several members of the group are getting together to share photographs and quaff a few pints, and that's all the incentive I need. An initial stop is made at Buckingham Palace to show QE2 my pictures and catch up, but a pack of Bobbies rebuffs me at the gate. They insist that she has been here the whole time and will not even deliver the duplicate photos I carried across the Atlantic for her to hang in the castle.

A hotel near the Earl's Court tube stop is my home base for a few days, and an extensive museum and pub crawl is initiated. The Tate, the Tower of London and the Globe Theater are visited, followed by stops at nearby taverns to contemplate modern art, bloody beheadings and iambic pentameter.

Later, London's rail system takes me to St. Alban's, a suburb north of the city, for a visit with Tony and Selena at a neighborhood pub. Sitting in a 500-year-old English village having a pint with Tony and Selena is a bit surreal. We downed our share of African lagers together, but the change of scenery from our last encounter, beneath Mt. Kilimanjaro's hidden summit, is kind of jarring. A soccer game is on the telly; a British girl takes drink orders and we are in a medieval square surrounded by Roman architecture from the 1500s.

Seeing how you get along with people you've only known from a vacation can yield awkward results, but our safari was more akin to a friendship pressure cooker, and we accumulated two years of stories in two weeks. The reminiscing is over in short order, and we pick up where we left off, riffing on every subject that comes up and making fun of Americans and their presidential elections.

A few nights later, I join Tony and Selena for the official reunion at a pub on Fleet Street called Ye Olde Cheshire Cheese, which was once frequented by a famous writer named Charles Dickens. The Earl is ancient and small, with five centuries of ambiance soaking in its warped walls. The pub is a maze of awkwardly shaped rooms, listing floors and head-butting doorways. While I wait for Tony and Selena, a club of octogenarian bridge players files into an adjacent room, and I cringe every time one of them trips over the unevenly terraced floor. Tim and Janet drive down from Leeds and join us at the bar. The Daft One is not included. Roy shows up briefly and insists on leading the group on a long hike through the rain-speckled streets to a bar from a more recent century. We rifle through photos and go to an elaborately designed restaurant in Covent Garden called Sorastro. They could stage operas in here if people weren't having their dinner; balconies drop from the ceilings, and turrets and gilded curtains separate eating nooks. Tony, Selena, Tim, Janet and I take a more leisurely stroll through our photos and discover that we have all the same ones, only from slightly different angles. The reminiscing is still early when the conversation hits the speed bump that is The Daft One. The group responds with audible groans and heavy eye rolling, except for Tim, who continues to display an otherworldly sympathy.

"He's not such a bad guy."

"Do we have to talk about him?" Tony says, refusing to allow The Daft One to ruin his vacation or his dinner. "I don't even want to hear his name."

He's right, of course. None of us would trade our African experience for a healthy version populated by rhinos and crystal views of Kilimanjaro. Now that the trip is over, the images that rise to the forefront are not of churning bowels or annoying roommates but of wildlife that made a zoom lens unnecessary and of laughing until our stomachs hurt. As stories are recounted and tales told, the zipping and hurling grow dim, and only the highlights remain. After six weeks removed, Ngorongoro Crater is not recalled so much for its rhino omissions but for how it was almost a perfect day.

After dinner, on the tube back to Tony and Selena's flat, I see an advert with the word *doddle* in the headline, a heretofore unheard-of British word.

"What does *doddle* mean?" I ask.

"Something that comes very easy," Selena says.

"You should have taught me that one."

"It never came up."

Minouk sends an e-mail. She survives Nairobi but still feels poorly upon her return home, and has been nauseous and diarrheic for several weeks now. She takes samples of an unspecified nature to her offices and has the lab test them. The results reveal that she suffers from *Giardia lamblia,* a protozoan parasite that comes from tainted drinking water. The parasite is a resilient microscopic cyst that acts as a suitcase for the infectious materials it carries. *Giardia lamblia* causes intestinal distress for a brief duration, including nausea, diarrhea, abdominal cramps and low-grade fevers. This particular parasite is a contagious bugger and can remain in your intestines for an indefinite period. This confirms everyone's suspicions as to the source of our ailment. It is The Daft One in Lake Manyara with the untreated drinking jug. Rest assured, I feel fine now. I will not infect anybody. Although, the saliva glands have been fairly productive lately. I have been feeling a little queasy—ugh. It's nothing, I'm sure. Really, nothing, erck . . . zip, hurl.

5016314R0

Made in the USA
Lexington, KY
25 March 2010